Blade Heart

The Tony Kenworthy Autobiography

Tony Kenworthy with John Brindley

Blade Heart
The Tony Kenworthy Autobiography

Tony Kenworthy with John Brindley

Vertical Editions
www.verticaleditions.com

First published in the United Kingdom in 2013 by Vertical Editions, Unit 4a, Snaygill Industrial Estate, Skipton, North Yorkshire BD23 2QR

www.verticaleditions.com

ISBN 978-1-904091-80-6

A CIP catalogue record for this book is available from the British Library

Cover design by HBA, York

Printed and bound by CMP (uk) Limited

To Jacqueline, Sofie and Wil, and all fellow Blades fans

Contents

Foreword by John Garrett, Sheffield United FC

I WAS fortunate to be born in Sheffield and as a Blade. I come from a long line of those devoted to the religion of Red and White who worship at the temple known as Bramall Lane, and it has given me many gods of the footballing kind to worship at-the-boots-of down the years.

My early games as a youngster are a bit of a blur. I know I was there – I had no choice as when my Dad couldn't take me to the Lane, my older brother (by some 20 or so years) was always happy to oblige. Both would try and keep me still long enough to point out some of the greatest players for both United and the opposition of the day. Sadly, playing a game of tiggy around the Kop steps and gangways generally won but, as the 1970s wore on, so did my awareness of those out on the famous field.

Bramall Lane is a special place – the oldest ground in the world to have staged professional football and the venue of many of other 'firsts' in the game; it's one of only two venues to have hosted both the FA Cup Final and Ashes Test cricket as well as the first ever floodlit game of football. It has always been a place where no player can hide. You can get away with a lot in the eyes of its educated crowd as long as you are simply prepared to lay your body – and indeed your life – on the line for the Red and White stripes. Show heart, courage, passion and commitment and you will be alright in their eyes. Add skill and finesse to the mixture and you are a potential Legend of the Lane

As my interest increased, so did my need for a personal

hero, someone who epitomised what I, as a youngster, wanted to see out on the pitch. John Harris's stylish side of the early 1970s was on the wane and 1975/76 saw United effectively relegated by Christmas. Money spent on the South Stand, which had risen over the famous cricket wicket, had diverted attention away from the fact that many of the great players were getting past their prime.

Blades legend Ted Hemsley had been castigated by manager Jimmy Sirrel earlier that season for telling him the only way the team could be prised out of trouble was to use the youth available, most notably TK, Keith Edwards and Imre Varadi. Sirrel ignored this prudent advice until the last – a major folly. TK was introduced to the first team on the bench at Manchester City on March 6 as the Blades were drubbed 4-0, before making his League debut at Norwich City on April 3 as United ran out 3-1 winners, one of the few bright spots in a dark season.

Tony is one of my heroes, as he is to many Blades of my age. His rise through the ranks and his cementing of a permanent place in the side corresponds very much with my own rites of passage. As I became old enough to begin travelling to away games with my mates, he was one of the driving forces in an ailing team. A player who would always answer the criteria for hero status, never letting either you or the club down. More than that, he was one of us.

I saw my Dad cry the day we went down to Division Four at the hands of Walsall. For reasons covered in this book, TK wasn't on the pitch to take the penalty that would have saved us. He sat there, head in hands, while the only one who had the guts to pick the ball up, place it on the spot and take the shot, sank to the floor as he failed. That said, the following season and its ultimate title win cemented a whole generation of fans, bonded together in the common cause of the Blades. There were many heroes, but one who stood out and gave his all was TK – that is a fact.

Tony could have achieved far more had he taken any one of numerous opportunities to leave Bramall Lane yet he turned advances down to stay where his heart was, a sentiment many a modern day player could do with taking on board. A well balanced player who could play on the left at either centre back or full back and as hard as nails, TK would walk into my all-time best Blades XI.

They always say you should never meet your heroes as you are liable to be disappointed. Tony is a total exception. I have been privileged to call him a friend for the best part of 15 years and he is everything you could wish him to be, living up off the pitch to what I thought about him on it.

Warm and funny, yet always brutally honest and self deprecating, TK's book is a great look behind the eyes of a modern day Blades hero and legend. His final departure from Bramall Lane then opened up another chapter as he wrote his name into Mansfield folklore with his winning Wembley penalty

His personal life and love of the Sheffield scene got him into more than the odd scrape and was followed later by a spell at Her Majesty's pleasure. It's typical of TK, the man, that he very honestly lifts the lid on what became a life-changing time for him.

I have been fortunate to hear many of these stories from Tony himself and I am sure, when you have had the pleasure of reading them, you will see what I mean. They really don't make them like TK any more. He is genuinely a top, top lad.

Thanks for the memories, TK!

Introduction
Welcome to Hell

EVERY BAR of *Tie a Yellow Ribbon Round the Old Oak Tree* acted as a fresh twist of a dagger to my shattered heart. My friend Mark and I sat next to each other on the coach alongside ten dangerous-looking strangers, scarcely muttering a word. His eyes were as wide as saucers.

Irony of all ironies, I was on my way 'home' to Leeds to a place I could still visualise very vividly from my upbringing. Dad drove me to Oldfield Lane on a Saturday morning to play for Leeds City Boys, passing this dank, eerie, grey castle-like building just off the main road. 'That's where you go if you do something REALLY bad,' he said. How those words made me shudder. Now I could no more get them out of my mind than the chorus of that song being repeated over and over again on the coach radio. It tells of a penitent man about to be reunited with his family, older and wiser after a bad experience. That was my story too, but not before I went through a personal nightmare 'inside' at Armley and Rudgate prisons.

I thought I'd gone through everything on the football field. I fell in love with Sheffield United as a teenager and discovered all the unpredictability and gut-wrenching dramas and disappointments of the sport as we went from the First Division to the Fourth – and almost all the way back again. Top clubs came calling but I wasn't interested, not even after we hit rock bottom THAT unforgettable day at Bramall Lane. I was very popular, at least in the Red and White half of the city, and lived life to the full off the pitch.

I'd have happily stayed there for ever but injuries caught up with me and I was packed off to Mansfield Town where I was as surprised as anyone to fulfil one of my football dreams.

One newspaper story apart, which I was virtually blackmailed into, I've never spoken of the four and a half long prison months that shaped the rest of my life. Not even to Mum and Dad who helped me through it, nor my lovely wife Jacqueline whom I met afterwards. Until now!

So this is a football book – and more. It's about the twists and turns in life of a Blades fan who took more than his fair share of knocks but always kept the faith.

Welcome to my story, the mostly honest and good and the occasionally dark and bad. Let's go back to kick off!

1

Echoes of Elland Road

THE HORRORS of prison were a million miles from my happy and settled childhood. Born on October 30, 1958 to parents Terry and Rita, I was raised in a three-bedroom semi-detached house on Redhall Crescent on the Cardinal estate, just a mile away from Leeds United's Elland Road. I was one of three children. Brother Terry bounced into the world three years earlier and sister Julie followed two years after me.

Mum and Dad met locally as their parents lived barely 150 yards from each other on the same estate. Difficult to believe, I know, but they weren't initially thought to be a match made in heaven as the Kenworthys took a fair bit of getting used to. I come from a line of good practical down-to-earth males who tackle life hands-on and tell things straight – and you wonder where I get it from? Grandad Harry was a lively sort – a busker who loved his cars, gregarious by nature. I'd pass his red vehicle in the morning and return after school to find he had repainted it blue. He was a true Mr Fix It who thought nothing of giving punters down the club a song when the turn didn't show, and produced a son who shared his love of getting stuck in and getting himself into harmless scrapes. Dad was a keeper of pigeons and chickens who had enjoyed life in the army. Serving in a German prisoner camp, he carried out his task of serving dinners to the Sergeants and other officers, but spat in them first to show them who was boss. Good lad!

Mum's side of the family, the Mitchells, were quieter by nature – hence the culture clash – but just as quirky when you got to know them. Mum's Dad, another Harry, was a character and a half. He was the bloke with the football gene who loved to come and watch me and was responsible, bless him, for the scrapbooks that helped so much in the writing of this story. Like the other Harry, he would give us a song, but in different circumstances. Working his bollocks off down the cotton mill during the week, he loved his drink at weekends. He went to the club for a few pints on a Sunday lunchtime, then slept on a bench waiting for the place to reopen in the evening. Many a time after I finished playing football, he came swaying over to give me a few words of wisdom, then a rendition of Poor Little Lamb. Sounds crazy, but it became part of 'normal' family life. There was no harm in the bloke and the sight of his wife, a woman of some 20 stones, carrying him home after one of his drinking sessions became another familiar and humorous sight we accepted without question.

When I came onto the scene the two sides had well and truly blended into almost an extended family. Dad was a traditional 9am to 5pm worker at the Moorhouses jam factory in Leeds and later employed by Cadburys as a forklift truck driver. Mum also worked at the factory and had spells at both Marks and Spencer and a pharmaceutical company. We were a run-of-the-mill Leeds family who made the very short move to Cardinal Square in the search for more living space after Julie was born.

My parents were great – still are for that matter. They didn't have much money, but the three of us never went without and were shielded from the stress Mum and Dad went through just to keep our lives ticking over. Dad did as much overtime as he could to bring in extra cash. Things were undoubtedly tight at times but my parents lived by the principle of not getting into debt. What we couldn't afford we didn't have, yet they usually scraped together enough for us to go on a week's break to either Butlins or Scarborough during the summer. Going abroad in those days was like going to the moon. Dad paid about £200 or £300 for a car, usually a Morris Minor or a Hillman Minx, equivalent to one of about £1,000 these days.

Both my parents are staunch Leeds United fans. Dad always loved his football although he only played at a local level. He was frustrated that his long working hours limited his opportunities to go to Elland Road to watch his heroes. But he always encouraged Terry and me to play. Dad was a Catholic, which was one reason why all three children went to St Anthony's School before going onto Parkside, an RC school just a five minute walk away, for our secondary education. Catholicism contributed to Mum and Dad taking their responsibilities to look after us properly very seriously. Mum liked to see me tag along with Terry, although big brother wasn't quite so keen. He clipped me round the ear as soon as we left the house because, given the choice, he'd have rather been with his own friends.

Living in Cardinal Square suited me just fine. Bang in the middle of the estate was a school with football and hockey pitches where the caretaker happily turned a blind eye to youngsters kicking a ball about during the evenings. Almost as soon as I got home from school I nipped over the fence and was out again having a game with children two or three years older. It was a good thing all round. Mum could keep an eye on me from the window and being knocked around by bigger lads gave me a useful introduction to the game.

I had my school pals but my world was soon split in two with football taking a big priority. Rather than spend time with my school mates, once out of class I preferred to play football with people I knew but wouldn't term as friends. It was the first of many social sacrifices in favour of the sport I loved.

For obvious reasons, I was also a Leeds fan. Don Revie became manager after Jack Taylor resigned in March 1961 and gave me memories of one of the greatest teams the domestic game ever produced. I vividly recall European Cup nights bringing rare live football to our TV, including the two legged Battle of Britain semi final against Glasgow Celtic in 1971. Unfortunately for the Kenworthys and Yorkshire, Celtic followed a 1-0 victory at Elland Road with a 2-1 success in the return at Parkhead, a match played in front of a record crowd of more than 136,000! More often, we huddled beside the radio to listen to a crucial game at home or in Europe. If really lucky, I was taken to Elland Road itself, sometimes being smuggled through the turnstiles and ushered to the front to get a good view. There and then I discovered the meaning of 'live' football. The feel and smell was tangible, the grass so green, it felt like a theatre. Those players were gods to me. Thanks to Elland Road I always know a 'real' football club when I see one.

What a team that was: Big Jack Charlton guarded the back door, snarling and snapping to ensure there was rarely a way through to the occasionally erratic Gary Sprake in goal; fiery Scot Billy Bremner blazed the midfield trail alongside that Irish magician Johnny Giles; and, in those days, they had wingers, too! I'll never forget the sight of Eddie Gray, shoulders hunched, leaving countless defenders in his wake and Peter Lorimer, the right winger with thunderbolts in his boots. Then there was 'sniffer' Alan Clarke, goalscorer supreme, hunting down the regular chances coming his way. That team won its fair share of trophies but should have had many more. The FA Cup final against Chelsea, in the same season as the Celtic tie, was a great example. It is widely acknowledged as one of the few outstanding cup finals, but how Chelsea scraped a 2-2 draw at Wembley before winning the replay 2-1 was a mystery.

In my young football life, I again followed in my brother's shadow. When Terry was 14 years old and I was 11, he played for a team called Redhall Juniors, run by Janet Clarkson. I tagged along with my kit on a Sunday morning hoping someone wouldn't turn up and they'd give me a game. Some of the lads were good players and thought I was too small. But a fair few changed their opinions by the final whistle. Terry was a naturally good footballer, a talented forward with enough creative flair to win trials with Blackburn Rovers and Mansfield Town. He could handle himself and never shied away from a fight. I was also a forward banging in my fair share of goals.

When playing for Oldfield Lane in Leeds I had trials with Leeds City Boys. The school sent lads there on the weekend for about 200 youngsters to be weeded down to 30 for the teams. I had the advantage of playing regularly with talented slightly older lads who were getting trials with some decent clubs. I went to places such as Liverpool and Manchester and have still got the reports to remind me I sometimes scored three or even four in a match. As an added bonus, I enjoyed a massive game on a Sunday on the school field. It was about 20-a-side with fathers and children playing together – a community event showing what great days they were to grow up in.

I wish I could be equally enthusiastic about my Roman Catholic school. Run by nuns, it was very strict and I didn't like it much. Going to the all-boys secondary school was no big deal as Terry marked my card. My fondest memory was of a teacher called Mr Rafferty who encouraged me to play football in the playground and said I was a good player. Parkside was almost on our doorstep and had a brilliant reputation for sport. Leeds and England defender Paul Madeley was just one of the sports stars who'd been a pupil there, along with several top rugby players. I enjoyed playing rugby and had trials with Leeds, being a good runner and relishing the physical side of the game which puts a lot of people off. Tackling and rough and tumble was right up my street and Dad encouraged me until he realised there could be a question over my future sporting allegiance. He needn't have worried, though, because football was always my number one.

I was always a middle kid as far as my school results were concerned, neither one of the brightest pupils, nor near the bottom of the class. Destined to leave with a handful of exam passes to my name, I never wanted to do anything else except play football. One interest I did enjoy was bird nesting as my father kept chickens. He liked us to be 'real' boys, go out and come back mucky.

Most parents thought the same way with little hint of the political correctness of today. Whatever I got up to, there was no chance of me getting too rebellious. I respected Mum and Dad's good example too much and wasn't the type to cheek them back. Dad took me everywhere to play football – I could never have become a professional without him. He just sat and waited in the car whilst I trained.

To a certain extent, Julie got her nose pushed out as Dad spent more and more time with me. I could well understand her being upset. He also began to lean towards me and my sport rather than Terry's. Although he had at least as much natural talent, Dad noted my brother didn't put in the necessary hard work after school. Whilst I spent three or four nights a week training, he preferred to be with his mates. We live in an age where young people sometimes expect instant success or fame – but shortcuts are rare. No disrespect to Terry, but dedication is often the difference. I'm a big believer that if you are going to do something then give it 100 per cent. Instead many lads go out and have a few drinks.

Perhaps realising he wasn't quite going to make it as a footballer, Terry made the huge and brave decision to leave home at the age of 17 with a mate and live in New Zealand. That was a major upheaval to all the family, not least to me. I was just 14 years old and we'd spent a lot of time together. He was my older brother and I naturally looked up to him, so it was a major loss that he was no longer around. Terry went on to combine working with playing decent football for North Shore in Takapuna and still lives there to this day.

I never wanted Terry to move but the plus side was Dad concentrated on me even more. I played for Leeds City Boys, was Yorkshire captain and turned out for a successful junior side called Pudsey. We wiped the floor with most opponents and, as we had a number of other Leeds City Boys in our ranks, football clubs began to take notice. When not playing up front, I was getting stuck in as a hard tackling midfielder. It wasn't until one of the Leeds City Boys coaches took me aside and suggested I'd make a better defender that I took the hint. That advice stuck for life.

I also got an early taste for taking penalties. At the age of 14 I took part in a national junior penalty competition with the winners getting the chance to go to Wembley. I was selected to take mine at Huddersfield Town's Leeds Road ground and got through to the next round by slotting nine out of ten against the Terriers' first team goalkeeper. That took me through to the Victoria Ground, Stoke, where England's 1966 World Cup winning goalie Gordon Banks was between the sticks. It was a really big occasion and I got to stay overnight in a nice hotel to prepare. I was pleased enough to score six out of ten past a legend of a goalkeeper but gutted that just one more would have taken me to Wembley.

Scouts came knocking when I was playing for Yorkshire. You can imagine how thrilled I was when Leeds took an interest and West Bromwich Albion, another First Division outfit, also wanted a closer look. Eventually I went to both Elland Road and Liverpool for talks but one approach stood out – and that was from Sheffield United. Scout Eddie Edwards was first to sell the Blades to me. I liked him because he talked to me on first name terms and spared time and effort to visit my parents and keep tabs on my progress. But it was when he took me to Bramall Lane that the penny dropped. That was football love at first sight, not quite as glamorous as Elland Road, but what a great football venue. Sheffield United was clearly a big, big club with a proper ground and good First Division players to match in the late 1960s and early 1970s. But, more than that, they were homely and friendly. I knew I'd be treated like a valuable young individual at Bramall Lane instead of being a number at Elland Road. Fortunately, Mum and Dad didn't put me under any pressure to choose 'their' club. Providing I was happy, they were happy. So I took my first step on the road to being a professional footballer by signing schoolboy forms for the Blades

2

Nice One, Sirrel

I'D LOVE to say that from day one I was one of the lads and it was plain sailing at Bramall Lane. But that would be wrong, very wrong. Instead I was soon fighting the first of countless personal battles just to keep my head above water. Most United schoolboys were from the city and played their early football there. Wednesday and the Blades divided all the young talent fairly evenly between them in those days. All well and good, you might think, except I was from Leeds! I'd played against some of these lads for Leeds City Boys, so wasn't one of them. Others formed cliques, or friendship groups, I was more often on my own. I could easily have given in and decided Sheffield United wasn't for me. But I liked it there for some reason so I set my stall out. If this was the way it was going to be, so be it. Nothing was going to put me off Bramall Lane.

One of the biggest challenges for a young lad of 16 was moving away from home for the first time. Apart from staying over in Sheffield during school holidays, I'd never been away from my parents in Leeds. Now I was lucky to find good digs in Donnington Road with landlady Joan Clarke, a young single mother. A couple of weeks later Keith Edwards, later to become a Lane legend, moved in too. He's a couple of years older so helped me settle into my new surroundings. I had good backing from Eddie, who remained a good contact and friend, and John Short, who did a number of jobs for Blades including a spell as assistant manager. John picked me up from my digs to take me to the ground and was someone I could talk to and keep me positive.

In those lonely early days, I played Northern Intermediate League football with apprentices such as Martin Turner and John McGeady, whose son Aiden is a current Republic of Ireland international. I was enjoying myself, but the moment of truth wasn't far off – would I be taken on as a professional? That's the massive day in any schoolboy footballer's life when you either get the 'thank you very much but we're going to have to let you go' speech or they welcome you into the fold as an apprentice. I remember being told my fate alongside a lad called Steve Hockey. He got the bad news – I got the good. Life's like that, I'm afraid, particularly in football where more than most fall by the wayside.

That was a big turning point. From an early age, all I'd ever wanted to do was become a professional. Now I was going to get my chance although I was still a million miles away from the first team and top players like Tony Currie and Alan Woodward. I cleared out the dressing room and got out of their way as quickly as possible. I didn't want to speak with them, to be honest, because they were in a different league. They were First Division gods, I was just a kid with a football dream.

That could so easily have ended very quickly as Blades manager Ken Furphy didn't rate me – and wasn't slow telling me so. After about four months Furphy gave me a severe dressing down, saying I couldn't head the ball and wasn't good at this or that. Instead he liked a lad called Kevin Lilley who played in my position. I'm not saying Furphy was a bad judge but he wasn't keen on fellow young

Blade Simon Stainrod either. The full back was an upstart who insisted he'd be better off playing up front but Furphy was convinced he should stay where he was. History proved him wrong on both counts.

I'm convinced I'd have been drummed out of the Lane had Furphy stayed in charge. Mind you, results weren't going well for the manager as a season that started with high hopes after just failing to qualify for a UEFA Cup spot the previous year, soon hit the rocks. A lot of attention was focused on our new £100,000 striker Chris Guthrie but things just weren't meant to be either for him or the team.

Early that season I watched us play my old favourites Leeds United at Bramall Lane when Guthrie hit the post with a header that could have set us on the way to a morale-boosting victory. Bad luck such as that can influence a whole season. Also key players including Woodward, Ted Hemsley and rugged Scottish defender Eddie Colquhoun, were coming towards the end of their careers at that level.

I wouldn't have wished it on the team but our continued poor run of results had a totally unexpected upside for me. Furphy got the sack and United brought in Scotsman Jimmy Sirrel who'd enjoyed remarkable success at Notts County taking them from the Fourth to the Second Division and become a virtual legend beside the banks of the River Trent. Not everyone saw eye-to-eye with Jimmy, or even understood much of what he said, but he obviously saw something in me that Furphy didn't and I'll always be grateful to him for that.

In the early days under our new Scottish boss, I mostly played for the youth team on a Saturday morning before watching the first team in the afternoon if they were at Bramall Lane. My youth team coach was David Turner who had played for Blackburn Rovers and then gone to America after his career was cut short by injury. He was a great coach, brilliant with the young lads, and just the sort of guy

I needed to help me settle into the club.

Another experienced man always good for the odd piece of valuable advice was Harry Latham, a former player who'd been at Bramall Lane for years and had the job of sweeping out the dressing rooms. What a character he was. Very often he'd energetically perform his duties in front of us with not a stitch of clothing on. His bits would be flying all over the place and I remember thinking 'Jesus, what's this guy doing?' when I first saw him. Then, gradually, I got used to him and realised he was just one of the characters who made Sheffield United Football Club the very special place it was. Probably in his sixties, Harry sat on the wall like a teenager watching us training behind the old Kop until Dave said 'come on, then' and he took his place on the field with us. He then booted the ball anywhere and everywhere, shouting out who his 'pass' was meant for! It was madness, but great fun nevertheless.

Two more absolutely priceless characters at Sheffield United during that time were laundry workers Peggy and Maud. They were salt-of-the-earth women who cheerfully went about their duties of making sure our kit was in working order, which wasn't the most exciting of jobs. They got their compensation however, by 'checking out' any new talent in the dressing room. Whenever the Blades made a new signing we got the message to Peggy and Maud and they popped in for a quick peep. Hiding behind the fact they needed to wash our kit, they got a bird's eye view of our new man in the raw which kept them happy for a while!

I enjoyed the odd chance to play for the reserves in the Central League on a Saturday afternoon. Reserve games were a lot more competitive then, whereas now a lot of clubs only play friendlies or run an Under-21 side. Back then, it meant facing up to some very talented opponents. With just one substitute allowed, players not in the first team squad stayed sharp by turning out for the second team, so I pitted my wits against some well known names including Joe Jordan of Leeds, and Arthur Albiston and Paddy Roche when I faced up to Manchester United Reserves at Old Trafford. I even have a copy of the teamsheet from a Central League match against Stoke City played on Saturday, November 15, 1975 with the legendary Sir Stanley Matthews being substitute on the Potters side when he was in his 50s. The teamsheet cost 1p, the memory is priceless.

After living in Joan Clarke's house for about a year, I moved to a property the Blades had taken over at Nether Edge with some of the Blades players. Strangely enough, the manager and his wife shared an annexe to the property – not that we saw Mrs Sirrel very much.

Living with the boss as well as playing for him subjected us still more to his strange ways. One quirk was bolting the door at 10.30pm sharp, whether or not all the lads were back home – only for our landlady Vera, more forgiving of young men's ways, to come down 15 minutes later to unbolt it again!

Around this time Edwards, who'd moved in with his future wife's parents, Stainrod and I tackled the task of learning to drive. We found a great bloke who ran his own driving school and block booked three hours on a Friday afternoon so we could all have lessons in his Avenger Estate. This guy had a heart of gold and the patience to match as he allowed one to drive and the others to sit in the back. Being footballers, there was no shortage of stick and laughter flying around when one of us made a mess of a hill start. I'd only had four or five lessons when I put in for my test which the instructor thought was a bit too soon but couldn't do too much about. I had an extra reason to get my driving show on the road as quickly as possible. For being an absolutely terrible driver was one of the manager's worst kept secrets. The thought of getting into the passenger seat and letting Sirrel drive me to Bramall Lane was far more daunting than playing football. I spent a fair amount of time with one of my Blades colleagues Jimmy Conroy getting the garage completely cleared out ready for the arrival of my first car – a Ford Capri that set me back a cool £1,600. Often Jimmy and I were playing a relaxing game of pool in the house when we'd hear the vibrations of the manager backing, or rather crashing, his car into the garage.

Believe me, I made as sure as humanly possible I got my car there before him and the door was securely closed before Sirrel made his way back from Bramall Lane, which wasn't too difficult as the boss worked longer hours than the rest of us. On one unforgettable occasion Sirrel smashed straight into the back of a poor driver on his way to work and spent most of the morning blaming Keith Edwards. In his curious logic, our young striker was totally to blame because the boss was too absorbed trying to work out how to make him a better player to fully concentrate on the road! That summed up Jimmy perfectly – totally besotted by football and the world's worst driver.

I don't think Sirrel could have done much to halt our relegation slide that season. The die was pretty well cast from the day he arrived with the only question being whether we'd be able to beat a record low of 18 points in the First Division held jointly by QPR and Leeds United. I never had an inkling our struggles meant the first team door was ajar, even after Sirrel gave me a run out alongside Scottish wing wizard Jimmy Johnstone in a County Cup tie against Doncaster Rovers at the Lane. That was a privilege because even being on the same training pitch as the former Celtic and Scotland flyer was an education, I can tell you.

He was coming towards the end of his great career when he arrived at Bramall Lane but his movement in training was incredible. He changed direction like a swift and did things to defenders, me included, that just weren't fair. We could never get near the bloke, let alone get the ball off him.

I spent more than my fair share of time with Jimmy as he was staying at the Kenwood Hotel and often had the job of picking him up in the morning to take him into Bramall Lane. Even at 9.15am he would have a half of lager in his hand and tell me pointedly I should never get like him. An absolute gem of a man, Jimmy had hit the slippery slope with alcohol which was very sad.

*****

My first sniff of first team action came in surprise circumstances. Blades coach Alan Hodgkinson told me to report to the ground in midweek to play in a match featuring a group of trialists. I did as I was told only to be pulled off by John Short after about 10 minutes wondering what that was all about. I got my answer on the Friday morning. Dad used to take me home then drive me back for the youth team match the following morning. Imagine my shock when Joan Clarke rang from my digs to say the Blades had been trying to get in touch. One of the first team due to play at Manchester City had been taken ill and they needed me to join the squad. Joan passed on the message that I should get myself to Maine Road.

Dad drove me to Manchester with the young guy in the passenger seat in a state of high excitement. Unsure where to park when we finally got near the ground, Dad was directed to a safe place by the police and we went our separate ways. I was substitute and never likely to get any nearer the action than watching alongside the manager on the away team's bench.

I'll always remember that day. It wasn't the best time for us to come up against City, a damned good side including big Joe Corrigan in goal and the darting skills of Dennis Tueart up front. They were still celebrating winning the League Cup at Wembley against Newcastle United the previous week, while we were rock bottom and already very close to having our relegation to the Second Division confirmed. Asa Hartford, the Scottish international once rejected by Leeds for having a hole in his heart, scored twice, big Joe Royle got one and Tueart netted the other with a virtual repeat of his overhead kick Wembley winner. But neither our 4-0 thrashing nor two more nasty surprises after the final whistle could ruin the experience. Unbelievably, Dad returned to find his car had been towed away even though he'd followed best advice, and I got fined £6 – a week's wages – for not being in the right place when the club contacted me.

My next near miss was at White Hart Lane where I sat on the bench alongside Cec Coldwell, our first team coach and one of the true Blades characters. Young Simon Stainrod made his debut up front and we got murdered 5-0 by Spurs who had Martin Chivers and Ralph Coates in their talented side. I was excited just to be on the bench watching players on both sides I was virtually in awe of, and not too disappointed when Cec whispered in my ear there was no way the manager was going to bring me on that afternoon.

It was still a big shock when I made my first team debut on April 3, 1976 at Norwich City's Carrow Road. When I found out I was in the 12, I went back to Leeds to the factory where my Dad was working just to tell him. Then John Short broke the even bigger news I was starting. I was very much on my own on the coach as the others, who all knew each other much better, settled into their card schools with Woody, as usual, having a fag. Nobody said anything much to me and it was no different when I roomed with Eddie Colquhoun, an aggressive defender with a jet black beard who looked like the guy from Popeye.

I don't think he muttered two words after our evening meal as he read a book whilst I sat on my bed watching TV. Then, without warning, Eddie closed his book at about 9.30pm and turned off the light and the TV. Not given any choice in the matter, I just slid silently into bed. Next morning followed the same routine as we both went downstairs for breakfast. Eddie was in front and I followed, looking more like his son than his defensive partner.

Arriving at the ground, there were messages from friends and family. There were about six or seven telegrams wishing me good luck from my parents, former colleagues from Leeds City Boys and one of my schoolteachers. I read them as quickly as possible because it was almost time to get into my gear. Very little was said about tactics before I went out onto the pitch. One or two of the lads told me to relax and enjoy the experience and Sirrel came out with a simple message. He reminded me I had a job to do, so just go out and do it – oh and get 'your pound of flesh' – the manager's way of saying he expected his players to compete physically.

Our defensive task looked massive, trying to contain the fearsome partnership of Ted MacDougall and Phil Boyer whose goals had taken the Canaries to the verge of qualifying for Europe. Somehow, however, they hardly got a kick as we upset the formbook with a terrific 3-1 victory. Guthrie, Stainrod with his first for the club, and Currie all scored in the first half as we took control. Colquhoun may have been quiet off the pitch but was a strong influence once we kicked off, pushing and pulling me in all directions. I had a few butterflies in my stomach but treated it in exactly the same way as playing in the Northern Intermediate or the Central League. I just concentrated on getting stuck in and doing my very best. After the game, there was no wild back slapping or high praise, just a few calm 'well dones' as if I'd done the job they expected all along. It was nice, however, to read the manager describe my performance as '18-carat, you had to look for the things he did wrong'.

That display was enough to ensure I retained my place for my Bramall Lane debut the following Saturday against

West Ham United, another side with Europe on their agenda. They came to town with Trevor Brooking, Billy Bonds, Frank Lampard and Mervyn Day in a side about to tackle German giants Eintracht Frankfurt in the semi final of the European Cup Winners' Cup. Nobody batted an eyelid when the Hammers led at half time but three goals in quick succession from Woodward, Guthrie and Stainrod helped us to a memorable 3-2 victory – only our fourth all season in the league but our second in succession.

Then came the biggest game of all in my First Division career, the midweek trip for the return match with Leeds United at Elland Road. Could we make it three unlikely wins out of three against the team I'd idolised? Madeley, from my old school, was back in the Leeds line up alongside the Gray brothers, Eddie and Frank, Trevor Cherry and Billy Bremner with the contrasting talents of Clarke and the unpredictable Duncan McKenzie up front.

The guy all the pre-match hype was focused on, however, was tough-tackling England centre half Norman Hunter. The press was full of the idea that being a Leeds boy and a left sided defender who also enjoyed the physical side of the game, I was 'the new Norman Hunter'. At first, it was an exciting thought but when the comparison got dug up again and again over the years it began to get more and more unhelpful. To be honest, I would have settled for being half as good as one of the very best defenders of his generation.

That was destined to be the one and only time we were on the same pitch and was a massive night for me for so many reasons. My parents were interviewed on the eve of the game, explaining that, although Leeds fans by nature, they'd be supporting me on the night. I could scarcely have been prouder coming out onto the pitch surrounded by players from both sides I had huge respect for. Everyone knows Leeds had a reputation for being a physical side but that didn't do them justice. Like most great teams, they could mix it when the opposition wanted to battle and play when that was the better option. In any case, you weren't likely to hear me complaining about a few meaty tackles.

There were no toilets in our dressing room and going into the corridor to have a wee before kick off, I heard the thudding sound of a football ricocheting around the walls – no doubt kicked by a home player in an effort to unsettle me. I also recall that familiar feeling of being dazzled by Leeds' ultra white shirts as we stood in the tunnel and I contemplated marking one of my idols, Alan Clarke. I'd watched the guy from the terraces and even been to Wembley when they were on the receiving end of a shock result thanks to a goal by my future Blades boss Ian Porterfield for Sunderland. It seemed too good to be true that here I was playing on the same pitch.

The manager had masterminded a famous 1-0 League Cup win for Notts County earlier in the season at Elland Road, a result that very possibly clinched the Bramall Lane job for him. I don't recall him mentioning that too much but we employed similar tactics of soaking up endless Leeds pressure and trying to catch them on the break. We had no choice as the home side battered our penalty area for most of the night. Goalkeeper Jim Brown, like the Magpies and Sunderland number ones before him, had an inspired night as we fought to stay in the contest until a memorable strike from Woodward edged us in front.

I picked up one of three First Division bookings in that mini-season and had no complaints. Generally it was a case of trying to adjust to a much faster tempo of first team football but on that occasion, it was a deliberate tactic to stop McKenzie. Signed by Brian Clough during his infamous 44 days at Elland Road, McKenzie was a very skilful maverick of a forward who could easily make defenders look silly. He skipped past a couple of Blades defenders and I decided he wasn't going any further. There was no such thing as 'the last man', so little danger I'd pick up any more than a caution for preventing Leeds carving out a good scoring chance. 'You'll not get very far in the game like that,' said McKenzie, picking himself up gingerly. We held on for our own famous 1-0 victory which felt like a cup final triumph. It was the perfect end to an unforgettable night for me.

Our great form couldn't last and a week later both the Blades and I were brought crashing back down to earth at Ayresome Park against Middlesbrough. Again, they had some terrific players in that side – Scottish midfield dynamo Graeme Souness, Liverpool's inspiration in the years ahead, Terry Cooper, the former Leeds and England full back, and David Armstrong, one of the best forwards in the division. But that was Tony McAndrew's day as he scored all three goals in Boro's comfortable 3-0 win and a very unfortunate one for fellow forward David Mills, who'd just been picked for an England squad. The two of us went haring after the ball and I caught him with a crunching tackle that broke his collarbone and resulted in him being taken off with his arm in a sling.

That could have been seen as a sending off to be quite honest but Souness did me a favour by arguing my case with the referee saying I was just a kid. Then, as he helped me up from the deck, he let me know who was boss by punching me as clean as a whistle in the stomach. There were no hard feelings from me though and Souness was a guy I really admired both as a great footballer and a very good manager. Sadly, Mills never got the England cap he probably deserved. I'd argue the tackle and the injury was just one of those things. Unlike the McKenzie incident, I didn't set out to foul him but was just naïve and late in going for the ball. Sirrel did me the favour of substituting me soon afterwards, concerned I was teetering on the edge of a dismissal that would have done me no good at all.

There were just two games to go and we managed to

round off the season and our stay in the First Division in style. A single goal from Guthrie saw off Newcastle United at Bramall Lane before Birmingham City arrived in town on a very important mission. Closest rivals Wolves had already completed their fixture list and Blues needed a point to overhaul them right at the end and maintain their own top flight status. It was a special night for Woodward, who received his Blades player of the season award before kick off and scored on his final First Division appearance to put us in front. It was a pretty emotional one, too, for Blues midfielder Terry Hibbitt who netted the crucial equaliser in a 1-1 draw to send his brother Kenny and Wolves down.

Again I was given the benefit of the doubt when, after being cautioned for a slide tackle, I was given a lecture by referee Peter Willis for bringing down Peter Withe, later a Blades colleague. A draw wasn't that bad a result against a side which included Kenny Burns and Trevor Francis, shortly to be European Cup heroes with Nottingham Forest, and brought down the curtain on an amazing few weeks. All of those six games, in which we won four and drew one, were a huge personal bonus. I could scarcely credit it that a 17-year-old lad on just £6 a week was mixing it in such exalted company. Equally, as I soaked up a fair amount of praise for my performances, I never thought they'd be the only games I'd ever play in the First Division.

*****

I got to know the manager's highly individual style quite well, and was in a good position both to appreciate the eccentric qualities that made him so successful at Notts in two spells either side of his time at Bramall Lane and why he didn't quite make it with us. The guy took his football deadly seriously and would go into the tiniest detail about Saturday's game for a couple of hours on a Monday morning. Then, with our minds still buzzing, he'd organise one of his endless practice games. This was fine for a youngster like me at the beginning of my career and eager to soak up everything like a sponge but irritating for Currie, Woodward, Colquhoun and others, who had seen it and done it in a league in which Sirrel was still a novice.

Don't get the impression, though, that I was established as one of the lads because I still had a long way to go on that score. During a close season tour of Gibraltar, where we took on Lincoln City and Wolverhampton Wanderers, I went out for a few drinks one evening with the rest of the lads. It was nice to feel part of the team socialising at last, problem was that when I looked around later in the evening all the others had gone! I was left on my own and didn't even know the name of the hotel in which we were staying.

I could hardly wait until August to see where I stood in the manager's pecking order and how we'd fare in the Second Division. The general impression among the local press, at least, was we'd be there or thereabouts in our bid for an instant return, but it wouldn't be easy. The main blows were that Currie had made his much expected move to Leeds United during the summer and Len Badger, another true Sheffield United legend, was also about to bow out. The question on everyone's lips was whether Sirrel had the guts to gamble on his talented youngsters, such as Stainrod, Gary Hamson and me, or scour the market for more experienced reinforcements

In the event, Sirrel was very loyal to us youngsters in our first season back in the Second Division – one which began with a fair deal of promise. We made a steady, if unspectacular, start although we suffered a real humbling at Brian Clough's Forest where we got whipped 6-1 by a side that went on to win the First Division title and the European Cup in the next two seasons. I was again up against the might of Peter Withe and got a first hand view of just how good that team was. On the right flank and having a particularly impressive game was a speedy youngster called Terry Curran, just beginning to make a name for himself in the Forest ranks. Much more about that young man later!

The Nottingham clash Sirrel was really looking forward to, of course, was with his old side Notts County who came to Bramall Lane just after Bonfire Night. A deserved 1-0 victory was a morale booster and lifted us to seventh place in the table. I was one of three teenagers in the side whilst Woodward, at the other end of his United career, was our skipper.

Clubs aren't always very co-operative when international sides come calling for their players, particularly when it isn't the senior side. Things weren't going that well for us as a side when England Youth asked Blades to release Stainrod and me for a tournament in Monaco. But, to his credit, Jimmy insisted it was right for both of us to go. 'The lads must have the opportunity of international honours while it is there,' he said. Thanks to Jimmy, I had the honour of not only representing my country but also being skipper in the tournament. The highlight was a 3-0 victory over Spain in which both young Blades were on the scoresheet. We were playing alongside some real stars of the future including Vince Hilaire, Chris Woods, Kenny Sansom and Sammy Lee.

Altogether I had the honour of sporting the three lions in two tournaments as I also took part in an event in Holland where Sansom, who became a full international stalwart, wore the armband. We remained unbeaten but a draw in our final game meant we didn't make it through our group. As a football experience, I couldn't have asked for anything better. Just as with my mini First Division career, the opportunity to represent my country never came along again, despite the kind things managers said about me. So I will always be grateful to Jimmy Sirrel for giving me that very special feeling of wearing an England shirt.

The manager played me in midfield early on that season which resulted in me losing my place. But Sirrel then gave me the perfect 18th birthday present – a recall for the trip to Cardiff City. I was going to play in midfield again, despite the loss of defender John Flynn to a broken leg, but an injury to Eddie Colquhoun allowed me to go back into my favourite position in Sirrel's team of teenyboppers. I may have just been coming of age but was actually only the third youngest Blade on show as record breaker Gary Hanson and Simon Stainrod, man of the match with both goals in our fine 2-0 victory, were both still 17. I was getting rave reviews from the local press as I then had good games in a 1-1 Bramall Lane draw against Orient and a very hard earned 1-0 win at Cold Blow Lane, Millwall, when we held firm against a late battering on one of the most hostile of grounds.

One of Jimmy's most notable signings was talented midfielder Chico Hamilton, who'd been part of Aston Villa's League Cup winning side just a few months previously. He was our goalscorer in another notable Bramall Lane scalp as we saw off promotion favourites Chelsea 1-0. We were definitely in with a shout as we went into Christmas in the top six only for successive defeats by three of the better sides, Bolton, Wolves and Luton, to send us plummeting back down the table. I found myself suspended and missing a big FA Cup third round date with First Division Newcastle United at Bramall Lane as a booking in a Youth Cup tie against Burnley took me over the points limit. Again I was praised in the match reports for my display in a game against a very talented Southampton side at the Lane. Here I was pitted against Peter Osgood, Ted MacDougall and Mick Channon, not bad for a Second Division strikeforce. England World Cup star Alan Ball was another big name in the Saints team as we finished up drawing 2-2.

I had a fun moment amid a generally bad night at Molineux in February where we were flattered to only go down by 2-1. Our goal was deflected by Colin Franks with a Wolves player on the line then putting the ball into his own net. To my surprise, however, the announcer gave the goal to me which would have been my first for Sheffield United. I responded by giving it the traditional clenched fist but knew I'd have to wait for a proper celebration.

We were beginning to struggle in front of our home fans as well, not winning at Bramall Lane for three long winter months and causing fears we might just face a relegation battle come the end of the season. Sirrel responded by recalling the veteran Ted Hemsley, another fantastic club servant, for his first game in 16 months as we lost 1-0 at Blackburn Rovers. I helped ease the pressure by creating one of the goals as we beat Cardiff 3-0 at home in early March to climb five points clear of the drop zone. Less than a fortnight later we got morale-boosting revenge on Forest when a young Edwards scored both in a 2-0 victory at the Lane.

This was the start of a remarkable spell for a striker destined to become one of the club's all-time sharpshooters. His 11goals in an eight-match spell ensured we were never again in serious danger. We did have the disappointment during this spell of losing 2-1 in the return against Notts County in which I conceded a controversial penalty for an alleged foul on speedy winger Steve Carter. The last few games didn't mean too much statistically as we were almost assured of a mid-table finish but were of great significance to a youngster still making his way in the side. The 2-1 home victory over Oldham Athletic in April was a match that lives in the memory for very good reason as this time I did score my first ever senior goal for the Blades. An Edwards header was sent back across goal by Colin Franks and there I was to score from close range. It was as good a feeling as if I'd scored with a 30-yard screamer, I can tell you. Mind you, even my celebration wasn't nearly as good as that of Keith

Edwards who almost went on a lap of honour after breaking a Blades record by scoring for the sixth game in a row in the first half – not bad for a 19-year-old. In the end, we finished 11th with 40 points from 42 games meaning the jury was still out on the manager who gave me my big chance.

Being a semi-regular in the Blades side that season was a huge growing up experience for me. This was my first taste of being in a professional football club's dressing room almost week in and week out. Believe me, it was sink or swim. There's no such thing as allowances for youth or anything else for that matter in a dressing room. It's a hard-as-nails, unforgiving place. You're dealing with a team full of egos behind four walls and there's no hiding place. If someone discovers a weakness in your make up they'll dig at it mercilessly, I can assure you. The choice is either to stand your ground and say your piece, or crawl into a corner and let everyone climb all over you. I was a teenager fast becoming a man but with plenty of rough edges. It wasn't until years later that I truly discovered just how many.

I was disappointed that the Blades board quickly lost patience with Sirrel after a poor start to the 1977/78 season. The Scot was sacked towards the end of September after which he again proved his worth by returning to Notts County and taking them into the First Division. Coach Cec Coldwell, a true Legend of the Lane, took caretaker charge whilst Blades looked for a new man. Cec was a guy I got on well with as he was always willing to chat and a Sheffield United man through and through. I have to admit though just how much Cec meant to the football club largely passed me by at the time. It was only when I looked back and took in the remarkable fact he made nearly 500 first team appearances for the Blades before going on to coach and temporarily take charge of the team that I realised just what an amazing bloke he was.

I did get jogged in the right direction by the brief return

of another well-known Blades player, Geoff Salmons, who arrived on loan from Stoke. He told me in the dressing room, 'You don't know how lucky you are. You don't know the tradition of this football club.' Over the years, that comment often comes back to me and still means a lot today. I'd like to take this chance to thank Geoff for those wise words which really were a big influence on my career.

During Cec's spell in charge, I had an experience I will never forget, facing the great George Best when he came to Bramall Lane to play for Fulham. Cec gave me the special task of man marking the world-famous Irishman. Again, I probably didn't quite take in the significance of the occasion but can now look back at the fact I played against one of the world's most famous footballers, as I did when England's 1966 World Cup winning skipper Bobby Moore lined up against us at Craven Cottage. I remember following Bestie into midfield and putting him on the deck with a clumsy challenge. The winger responded by picking up the ball and tossing it at me in frustration, with the referee calling us over for a short talk. We managed to win 2-1 and if Bestie rolled back the years with a few brilliant moments towards the end, the hero that day was our own Chico Hamilton. He brought us back into the game after we'd fallen behind for the first time under Cec with a classical header before Woody netted our well deserved winner.

My fond memories of that great afternoon aren't limited to the 90 minutes however. Mum and Dad and Grandad all came to watch me and were in the players' lounge afterwards when the great man walked in. Bestie ruffled my hair, shook my hand, and bought all my family members a drink, a fantastic gesture I will always treasure.

The Fulham victory capped a fantastic October for the lads under Cec and we went unbeaten for eight games in all before losing 3-0 at Charlton Athletic. Even a broken bone wasn't going to keep me out of the side if I could help it.

I felt a sharp pain in my hand after falling on it during a 1-0 home victory over Oldham Athletic in November but it wasn't discovered until a full two months later. I fell on the same part of my hand again and Cec booked me in for an x-ray which showed the break. But, rather than risk losing my place, the consultant surgeon fitted me up with a lightweight plaster cast to wear when I went into battle. Cec also experimented with a midfield role which I never felt totally comfortable with. In the 2-0 home victory over Blackburn Rovers, I was given the task of man marking their playmaker Tony Parkes out of the game which I managed to the boss' satisfaction when he spoke to the press afterwards.

My other highlight of playing under Cec was that football rarity, an afternoon where almost everything goes right. Blades fans of a certain age will recall with great pride that we went to Ninian Park, Cardiff, and smashed the home side 6-1. It was an even more memorable match for me as I was among the goalscorers alongside Bobby Campbell (2), Woody, Cliff Calvert and Chico Hamilton. It was the sort of match legends and myths are made of and I'm sure many Blades fans thought they were watching Brazil. But the game was never that one sided – it was just one very rare occasion when virtually everything we hit ended up in the back of their net. In fact we earned a rollicking from the boss at half time even though we were 3-0 up before I smashed in one of my very best goals from outside the penalty area to make sure there was no chance of the Welsh side hitting back in the second half.

We also did well to go toe-to-toe with Glenn Hoddle and Steve Perryman, just two big names in the Tottenham Hotspur side we held to a 2-2 draw at Bramall Lane. Cec's chance of landing the job full time faded, however, as we then went through a nightmare three-game spell in which Arsenal beat us 5-0 on our own pitch in the FA Cup before Bolton and Sunderland also sealed wins against us in the following two league matches. A 4-0 defeat at Kenilworth Road against Luton Town was probably of still greater significance as the Blades opted to bring in big Harry Haslam as our next manager. The guy established a name as large as his physical stature by leading the Hatters into the First Division so there was a buzz around Bramall Lane wondering what he could achieve at a far bigger football club.

3

Don't Cry for Me, Martin Peters

WE were in for a big shock in the weeks that followed. For happy Harry Haslam was a lovely, lovely man but never truly the manager of Sheffield United. After getting used to a tracksuit boss in Jimmy Sirrel, a constant figure on the training ground with his endless practice games between the first team and the reserves, it was a huge culture shock to discover Harry was the exact opposite.

I'm not exaggerating when I say he never came to the training ground. There were no in-depth team talks or tactical get-togethers. The only time we saw him was about 15 minutes before kick off when he nipped into the dressing room rather like a chairman and basically wished us the best of luck for the 90 minutes ahead. He gave us a few pats on the back, relaxed us with a couple of light-hearted comments, and sent us out for the most important business of the week knowing Danny Bergara had done all the hardwork. It was a strange way of going about things that probably had its roots in Harry's spell in charge at Kenilworth Road where he had both Bergara and David Pleat working with him. His unorthodox methods had produced results in the past so we didn't ask too many questions and just got on with it.

The main bonus was Bergara was a brilliant coach. The Uruguayan was a believer in the beautiful game and a pleasure to work for. The fact we never got the results we were looking for under his leadership didn't detract from my view that he was a bloke years ahead of his time. Without having a go at any of my Blades team mates, Danny's methods were probably better suited to players at the very top end of the skill scale like Luis Suarez and Dennis Bergkamp rather than more modestly talented lads playing in the Second and Third Division. He concentrated on the finer skills of the game and would go ballistic if I brought the ball down in a lazy way in training. I felt really sorry for Danny for several reasons. Because Harry Haslam was nominally the manager, he was never going to get the recognition he deserved for the work he did. To make things still harder, Harry was always there in the background, a benevolent uncle figure the players could go to if we had a problem. Often players were disciplined by Danny only for Harry, not involved in what had gone on, to overturn his decision.

That mini-season under Haslam and Bergara, saw us smash five past Millwall and four against his old club Luton to gain some revenge for the beating they'd given us under Cec. But there were disappointments, too, rounded off by Cardiff gaining some revenge with a 1-0 victory at Bramall Lane. So, thanks mainly to a very good record at Bramall Lane where we claimed 13 of our 16 league victories, we again ended the 1977/78 season in mid-table.

It was enough for the new manager to mark my card. We were in Switzerland and Italy for our summer tour in July 1978 when Danny took me aside and said Harry didn't really fancy me. That was the first I'd heard of it as I'd been a regular during the last few games of the season, yet it worried me enough to seek a chat with Harry in the hotel. To my disappointment, he confirmed what his assistant had said before pointing out that Watford, whom future England boss Graham Taylor had guided into the top flight, were keen to take me. The situation changed, however, when I had a couple of decent games on tour. Danny, who always seemed to support my cause, said I'd shown just the qualities he'd been talking to the manager about. Better still, Harry then told me politely to forget our previous little chat. Staying at Bramall Lane was just fine and could even have resulted in me lining up in the same side as a certain Diego Maradona of all people as Harry opened his contacts book.

We were just beginning to see foreign players coming into the Football League with Harry playing a role in attracting Argentina World Cup winners Ossie Ardiles and Ricardo Villa to Spurs. Suddenly, two Argentines were on their way to Bramall Lane – midfielder Alex Sabella and a forward called Pedro Verde. Harry's original target had indeed been young Maradona but Blades refused to up their offer from £400,000. Would have been worth a few more pennies in hindsight, don't you think? Yet you can only imagine how excited the red half of the city was at bringing in two foreign stars including Sabella for a cool £160,000.

I was excited, too, but soon had my reservations. Verde, whose main claim to fame in retrospect was that Juan Sebastan Veron, later of Argentina and Manchester United fame, was his uncle, proved too lightweight for English football and only played a handful of games. There was more than a hint of the same thing about Sabella, although his football ability was never in doubt. Looking back now, his silky ball skills weren't the ideal fit for playing on terrible pitches in bleak winters, particularly when we went down to the Third Division. But one particular quirk made his life a lot harder at Bramall Lane. He never played or trained on a Friday for some reason back home and wasn't going to change that in England. Alex was a genuinely nice guy and I have nothing against him as a person. But, let's put it this way, his understanding of English was good until the word 'Friday' came up. He just shrugged as if he didn't know what they were talking about. There was bound to be animosity towards our star player enjoying his day off when the rest of the lads were soaked by rain or chilled to the bone in training.

Haslam, who increased our foreign contingent still further the following summer by bringing in a Dutch winger called Lenny De Geoy, also swooped on his former club Luton Town for striker Peter Anderson in one of his better moves. He was a genuinely good player and a witty man whose company I thoroughly enjoyed in the dressing room. Ando grabbed a debut goal in a victory over Luton Town and later scored our goal of the season – a sensational solo effort in the 3-2 Bramall Lane success over Sunderland. There was more competition, too, for my place in the back four as we now had Andy Keeley, signed by Cec Caldwell from Spurs, who could also play in midfield.

The season started painfully as I suffered a knee ligament injury in a 2-2 draw at Preston North End keeping me out of our big night early on that campaign, the visit of mighty Liverpool to Bramall Lane for a midweek League Cup tie. I sat in the stands as our lads pulled off the most unlikely of 1-0 victories to give our supporters hope we were in for a good season. Gary Hamson scored our goal but I swear that for the other 89 minutes, Kenny Dalglish and co had the ball without somehow being able to blow our house down.

I was back in the side when we drew another plumb home tie against Leeds United in the next round. That was a night I was really looking forward to – another chance to play against my boyhood club – but it turned out to be a more memorable one for a celebrated former Blade. Tony Currie returned to Bramall Lane with a lot of media attention on his dual with his successor, Alex Sabella. TC had the first laugh as he put Leeds into the lead with a stylish finish and Eddie

Gray (2) and Frank Gray rubbed our noses in it as they ran out 4-1 winners. Chris Calvert grabbed our consolation.

There were definite signs of hope with four-goal wins at home against Burnley and Oldham Athletic and that exciting victory over Sunderland but plenty of disappointments too. I came across a decision almost ahead of its time as we went down 2-0 to West Ham United at Upton Park. Trevor Brooking smashed a close range shot against my hand and I was so angry about the harsh penalty award I had to be physically restrained from confronting the referee. That kind of decision is given far more often now and is one I still argue with. Pop Robson got both the Hammers' goals from the penalty spot after goalkeeper Steve Conroy had done his level best to keep the dominant home side at bay.

I did my best to prove myself to Haslam in what was fast becoming a tense battle against relegation. One of my finest hours came at Burnley in March where I had a particularly good game and set us on our way to a priceless point with a thumping header from a John Flood corner, the 1-1 draw leaving us just clear of the bottom three.

There was no justice in the world the following Saturday as I picked up a very unusual booking in a 0-0 home draw against promotion contenders Stoke City, that was a far better game than the scoreline suggested. We were awarded a free kick which I was going to take only for one of their players to continue to stand just a few yards away. I withdrew from taking it thinking the referee would tell him to retreat the full 10 yards but was amazed when he flashed a yellow card in my direction! I hold my hand up and admit I deserved many of my cautions in my first few seasons – but that wasn't one of them.

Soon afterwards, I battled through five stitches in an injured knee to see us through to a scrappy but important 1-0 home victory over Bristol Rovers which set us off on a good run. We gave ourselves a chance of escaping a second relegation in three seasons with four wins in five matches, scoring plenty of goals, too, against West Ham, Notts County and Newcastle at St James' Park. It was personally very satisfying to beat the Hammers 3-0 after events at Upton Park, although the fans probably got more enjoyment from seeing Jimmy Sirrel's side thumped 5-1 on his first return to Bramall Lane.

Mickey Speight scored a brace for the first time in his career and sent out a public message that we weren't going to roll over easily. We had Bruce Rioch, the former Derby County and Scotland midfield star, giving us extra quality in an important area after signing on loan on transfer deadline day. Rioch got his name on the scoresheet in a morale-boosting 3-1 victory at St James' Park where my mate Anderson rounded off the scoring in the closing minutes. Having players of their ability on board was a major boost and Rioch quickly showed Bramall Lane fans he'd brought his shooting boots with him with a cracking 25-yard free kick in a tense 1-1 draw with Wrexham. The Welsh club's goalkeeper parried the ball out and I stuck it away for our equaliser after the visitors had led through an own goal.

My other main memories from that season, however, were the two matches against fellow strugglers Charlton Athletic – games I still laugh about with my mate and former Addicks striker Paul Walsh. We made the trip to The Valley a couple of weeks before Christmas where we went down 3-1. I had my hands full trying to stop Walsh, whose movement was truly exceptional as I told United reporter Tony Pritchett afterwards.

When Charlton arrived at Bramall Lane for the return match, my defensive partner John MacPhail was more concerned about their other main striker, a dark curly-haired gypsy-like character called Derek Hales. They'd been at it hammer and tong for virtually the whole of the 90 minutes in a previous encounter and that wasn't going to be forgotten with Hales in the Charlton line up for a match with both sides desperate for points to stave off relegation.

You couldn't meet a nicer bloke off the pitch than MacPhail, but he glazed over at about 2.45pm and became a totally different animal. His 'party trick' was to go into an aerial challenge leaning over the opposition player with his knee up. As the forward hit the floor, he came down full weight and stamped on his oponent. On this occasion, he attracted my attention before kick off and told me he was going to 'do' Halesy. I should either set him up or at least be ready for the big moment. That happened when Charlton had a goal kick. The two players were lined up perfectly as Hales rose to try to flick it on. MacPhail timed his challenge just right. He kneed his man as they went up for the ball and, after heading the ball away, fell straight on top of him, making sure the Charlton striker felt the full impact.

What happened next was pure football theatre. Hales drew his fist up from the floor and swung the most menacing punch you'll ever see on a sports field, missing MacPhail by inches. But what did the referee, who was in perfect position, do? He ran past and said: 'Oi you two, fucking behave' and that was it! You'll never get a better example of the way the game has changed disciplinary wise than that. I swear today both players would see red with MacPhail getting a three or four game ban and Hales probably twice as many. The Charlton game, which finished 2-1, kept us in the hunt to survive as were still in the bottom three but only on goal difference with two games in hand over the Londoners.

More typical of the overall season was our next visit to the North East when I nudged us ahead from an early corner at Roker Park only for us to get thrashed 6-2. I say thrashed because in many ways that night was the opposite side of the coin from the Cardiff game the previous season. We contributed plenty with Sabella scoring a brilliant individual goal and had many chances to add to our tally as I was one of three Blades players to have efforts cleared off the line in one goalmouth scramble and we also missed a late penalty. But most of the breaks went the way of the Roker men as they continued their march towards eventual promotion alongside Brighton and Stoke City. Their haul included a couple of penalties of their own, one after I committed a foul in a one-against-one with Conroy.

Successive 1-0 defeats inside four days by Blackburn Rovers and Cambridge United were hammer blows, leaving us going into our final battle with a talented Leicester City side on a Tuesday night needing to win by three clear goals to stay up. I had plenty on my plate dealing with a young Gary Lineker and it soon became clear that, despite our best efforts, we weren't going to do it. The final whistle blew on a 2-2 draw and the unthinkable had happened again – we'd gone down, this time to the Third Division. I hadn't felt the full force of relegation under Sirrel as it was inevitable before I even got on the pitch, but now I experienced that awful draining feeling of being involved in failure. The fans hate it, club officials hate it, as their jobs are often on the line, yet players don't always take it fully on board. Having already taken to Sheffield as a city and Sheffield United as my team, it hurt me to the core.

I recall with real pride the number of personal letters I received from Blades fans in the weeks that followed, thanking me for my efforts and hoping I would stay. That had a big influence on my morale and I've still got some of those kind letters. They needn't have worried as I had no intention of quitting Bramall Lane. Another personal consolation was being voted Blades Player of the Season for the first time. It's always special being honoured by the fans, the people who pay their money week in, week out to see you play. This one left me with mixed feelings. I didn't want to be tagged 'the best out of a bad bunch', as some suggested, but drew strength from knowing I'd put my personal house in order.

I admit getting selected for the first team so early did go to my head and I was drinking and eating too much during my first mini-season and the next one under Jimmy Sirrel. That played a part in me going into the referee's notebook too often and gaining myself an unwanted reputation. I was just that little bit slower off the mark than I should have been and was catching players rather than winning the ball cleanly in the tackle. But, during our relegation season of 1978/79, I kept off booze for a full year, cut down on the food and even took up squash. I was fitter and better for it and that was reflected both in my performances and fewer cards from officials. It was a massive shame we couldn't have been more successful as a side with the talent we had at our disposal.

*****

Rumours were circulating that another step down may be one too many for Sabella, particularly with Sunderland and Leeds United interested in his signature. Being relegated to the Third Division was a big body blow to a club of Sheffield United's stature. I'd known the club as a First Division or occasionally prominent Second Division side and here we were having slipped a long way down the football ladder. We'd been expected to do well in the Second Division, so you can imagine how highly fancied we were to thrive under Harry in the Third, where I would clash on the field for the first time with Sheffield Wednesday.

It didn't take me long to realise this was a very divided city and it was always going to be extra important for Blades fans that we got the better of the Owls. That hadn't been an issue during my first few years at Bramall Lane as Wednesday had been stuck in the Third Division for a few seasons before raising expectations of an overdue revival by appointing another England World Cup legend Jack Charlton as the new manager at Hillsborough. Signing Terry Curran from Saints was another Owls coup.

Being a Blade wasn't a cradle-to-the-grave affair with me as it is with many thousands of good Sheffield folk but I soon got to realise one city truth – you're either a Blade or an Owl – you can't bat on both sides.

Loving one and strongly disliking the other is the way of the Sheffield world, always was, always will be. There are two big football clubs, the Blades being biggest, of course, who compete every season, not only to be as high up the Football or Premier League as they can, but also to be better than each other. We can't pretend we like each other, so why try? If Blades lose on a Saturday, I'm sick. If Wednesday lose as well, that's consolation. That's all positive and above board as far as I'm concerned. Yes, of course, there's a line to be drawn, and that's where abuse, even violence comes in.

I remember following a bus in Sheffield once and reading the message 'Kenworthy is a wanker' daubed in paint on the back. That shook me up a bit. Firstly, it's not true and, secondly, it's not called for. People could dislike me as a footballer and I may not be everyone's cup of tea as an individual but I'm an honest human being. I won't call you a wanker, so don't call me one! It's worse still when heated emotions spill over into violence and I can't defend that either. Yes, I liked to freshen my direct opponents up a bit, but I never set out to hurt people. I don't want to see that kind of thing happen off the pitch either. Standing your ground and fighting your corner verbally is one thing, being a thug is another.

There was other local interest with Rotherham United, Chesterfield and Barnsley all being in the same division but no doubt at all what the fans were thinking about once the fixture list was announced – a little matter of a Boxing Day clash between the city rivals at Hillsborough. That, however, wasn't on the players' minds in the early months of the season as at long last we gave our long suffering fans something to smile about. We made a modest mid-table start but then went on a run of nine wins in ten matches to roar to the top of the table and open up a useful four point lead.

Things were definitely going for us during that spell and I had my share of good fortune too, when my left wing cross against Blackpool at Bramall Lane hit the far post and went into the net to add to my goal tally. To make it still sweeter we breezed past the Seasiders 3-2 at Bloomfield Road a fortnight later to complete a useful double.

We were doing well against our local rivals as we beat Barnsley at Bramall Lane before going to both Mansfield Town and Rotherham and beating them on their own patch. One of my memories comes from another away victory as I slid in at the far post to give us the lead at Gigg Lane, Bury, where we eventually won 2-1.

We weren't necessarily turning in five-star performances every week but were grinding out results and putting ourselves into a useful position before thoughts turned to that festive battle. The long build up to the big game began about three weeks before Boxing Day. If Christmas had been cancelled that year in Sheffield, I swear most of the city would never have noticed. All anyone wanted to know about in the pubs and clubs and the local media was the long awaited reunion of the two deadly rivals.

I can honestly hold my head up high and say the only thing on my mind was to go to Hillsborough that chilly morning, beat the hell out of our blue and white rivals and pick up two more points to increase our lead at the top. Kick off was brought forward to the unearthly time of 11am on police advice and we were as well prepared as possible.

We stayed overnight at the Kenwood Hotel, close to Bramall Lane, and as I woke up that morning and put aside the noise of John MacPhail's snoring, I went for a short walk in very good spirits. Even the short trip to Hillsborough was unique. Our coach had the difficult task of navigating through what seemed like the whole of Sheffield making its way to the ground. Being a holiday there was no public transport so supporters either had to drive, or walk. Fans of both sides didn't bother about inconvenience – they just wanted to be there for the first steel city derby. In the end we were grateful for our police escort or we'd have struggled to get there in time.

History books recorded that game as a record Third Division crowd of more than 49,000, but there were many more than that. A better estimate was 60,000, with about 15,000 more locked outside. I could feel, as well as hear, the cracking atmosphere in the ground and couldn't wait to get started. The pitch had a covering of thin ice. I was well up for it. But what happened next amazed me. We didn't live in airy-fairy politically correct days when players ready to kick seven bells out of each other start with phoney pre-battle handshakes, so why referee Pat Partridge told the teams to walk out together – a custom reserved for the FA Cup Final – was beyond me. Perhaps he hoped it would calm down the atmosphere between the two teams and their fans. He was sadly disappointed.

All hell was let loose in that tunnel including lads who weren't even playing. I regarded it as my chance to get my 'free one' in early and there were soon a series of fights breaking out between rival players before Partridge saw sense and ordered us back to our dressing room. MacPhail had a gentle word with Curran about what he was going to do to him once the game started. Fisticuffs may have finished fairly even but, for my money, odds swung in Wednesday's favour in that ugly scuffle. I looked at Sabella, the star midfielder Harry expected to play us to victory, and knew we'd be playing with ten men once we got on that pitch. The young man's eyes were as wide as saucers. A freezing Sheffield Boxing Day morning was never his cup of tea anyway but he was well and truly psyched out by what he'd seen. Wednesday were more than happy to sacrifice anything Jeff King wanted to do creatively to ensure Sabella wasn't at the races and our loss was always going to be greater.

Why Harry didn't spot the obvious signs we weren't all on the same wavelength as King launched into an early scything tackle on the Argentinian, I'm still not sure. His only excuse was that we still had a single substitute back then, so making a tactical replacement so early would have been a major gamble. As it turned out, such action would have backfired as skipper Mickey Speight went off with broken ribs early in the second half.

Myth and Wednesday legend has it that the 90 minutes belonged entirely to them. It didn't. Football matches don't always reflect the final result and we should have been walking back into our dressing room at half time in good spirits. Yes, lanky Owls striker Ian Mellor gave them the lead with a corker of a shot from about 25 yards, but we responded quite well.

A crucial match-turning incident shortly before the break summed up our miserable morning. Striker Jeff Bourne hit the bar and most Blades fans in that huge seething crowd would have put their mortgage on MacPhail equalising from the rebound. How big Bob Bolder kept the shot out I still don't know. I'm pretty sure he didn't. The Owls goalkeeper looked to be in no position to do anything about it but somehow got his bulky body in the way and we trooped off for half time, still a goal down instead of level at 1-1 but with a significant momentum shift in our favour.

I can't argue about what happened afterwards. It was all Wednesday in the second half and they rubbed our noses in it big time. Curran got himself a goal and had a hand in the other two as well as taking the mickey as only he could get away with. Fellow Blades fans know the facts and you don't need me to go over them in any more detail. Let's put it this way: Wednesday fans have dined out on that match for more than 30 years because it was a huge game for them, while we'd been playing huge games in the big divisions for years.

Looking back on it now, I can see Wednesday had another edge that day. There were more truly local lads in Big Jack's side who didn't need motivating to play against Sheffield United. We had our fair share – I was one of them – but we also had young lads who probably weren't quite so tuned into the importance of the occasion. I could hold my head up after Star reporter Tony Pritchett made me Blades man of the match for my display in our hard stretched back four, but that was no great consolation when my team had taken such a painful beating.

What hurt even more was that we failed to pick ourselves back off the floor that season. How much our slump in the second half of 1979/80 was a direct reaction to our defeat on Boxing Day I don't know. But it must have had a strong psychological affect on our boys because, after a couple of reasonable results immediately afterwards, we never regained the form that took us to the top.

A sign of the way the gods were beginning to turn against us came the following month at Exeter City, where we found ourselves two crazy goals down inside the opening three minutes. First came from an own goal when our defender Tony Moore tried to duck out of the way of a cross after just 15 seconds and ended up deflecting it into the net. Then the home side scored a 'worldy' from 30 yards and we were left with a mountain to climb before we'd even got going. To make things worse, John Matthews was sent off towards the end as we went down 3-1.

Haslam did his best to laugh that one off and also went

public to praise me for how I was shaping up. He said the Tony Kenworthy he first met wanted to fight rather than beat opponents and that if he'd wanted to find a world heavyweight champion, he wasn't about to scour Bramall Lane for one. But he wasn't nearly as jovial after a nervy 1-0 home victory over struggling Mansfield Town a few weeks later. He sensed this was no blip, but a full-scale fall from grace.

I did achieve a 'first' in February against Oxford United, netting from the penalty spot. Jeff Bourne, the former Derby County striker, was our regular spot kick man and there was general surprise among the Blades media when I stepped up and struck a low shot into the corner of the net, sending their goalkeeper the wrong way. I'd always fancied taking penalties from my schooldays and that shoot-out against the great Gordon Banks because I had a good shot on me. Whether it was my first penalty or my last, there would always be about ten seconds for a sharp intake of breath when the kick was awarded when I probably wished I was anywhere but there, then I'd pull myself together and focus on putting the ball exactly where I wanted. That success at the Manor Ground was enough to earn us a 1-1 draw. When asked afterwards by journalists why I'd taken the penalty, I told them honestly 'because I was the nearest player to the ball'. Simple as that.

Nevertheless we slipped from title favourites to promotion long shots before the return derby match at Bramall Lane began to occupy our minds. I went out of my way to talk with the lads in the weeks before that Easter clash to remind them they owed our fantastic fans a great performance. This was payback time, as far as I was concerned. Our supporters had taken three months of stick because we had failed to perform at Hillsborough and we needed to win on our own pitch to give them something to smile about.

I got myself involved in a public spat when interviewed

on Radio Hallam a couple of weeks before the game. I thought I was on safe ground chatting with DJ Ray Stewart who I knew very well and even did jingles for. But when the discussion got thrown open for phone calls from the public it got a bit more tasty. I took the bait and said I'd bet any Owls fan £50 that we'd win the match and gain revenge for Boxing Day. Even Ray was amazed at what followed. The switchboard literally jammed with Owls fans queuing up to take me up on it. He told me I should be careful, and not taking up any of the bets at least saved me a good deal of money!

Bramall Lane at Easter promised to be a much better stage for Sabella to show his talents. We were banking on him to rule the midfield whilst we planned to give Wednesday a taste of their own medicine. They sat on our star player at Hillsborough. This time Curran wasn't going to get a kick, apart from up the arse from me. Before Saturday, we still had one small matter to get out of the way – a long trip to the seaside to play Southend United on the Friday!

Yes, I know, it would never happen now and younger readers probably find it hard to believe it happened then but I had no complaints. I wanted to play football and Southend was no exception. Problem was our star player didn't see it that way. This was Sabella's ultimate no-no – football on a Friday. Harry picked him for that trip but it didn't surprise any of us that he didn't play. We travelled to Essex on the Thursday and I remember waiting at Bramall Lane for one last player before we boarded the coach. Nobody had a clue where Sabella was as we waited patiently for his car to arrive. His home phone kept ringing with no answer and, with no such thing as a mobile, we had no other way of getting in touch with the Argentinian.

Fact is, Sabella didn't turn up so we played Southend without him and lost 2-1. Disappointing but it could have been worse. I was in agony with a broken toe as we set off for South Yorkshire and Pritchett reported I was injured and out of the derby match against Wednesday. No way. I wasn't going to let the small matter of broken bones stop me. I had yet another injection to numb the pain and declared myself fit to tackle my special job the following day – sort out Curran. His Hillsborough heroics apart, this guy was a First Division player who stepped down a couple of divisions to play for Wednesday. Everyone knew he was their dangerman so we couldn't afford him to take centre stage again.

You'll probably find it shocking that Alex Sabella was on the Blades teamsheet. Harry hated confrontations and dealt with it in a fairly typical way. He told the press Sabella was injured for the Southend match, but was fit and ready to go against Wednesday. All the lads knew that wasn't true but the boss was gambling on his big signing producing the goods when it really mattered. Playing on a Bramall Lane pitch like a billiard table compared with frosty Hillsborough prompted Haslam to think we would see the real Sabella. The crowd wasn't quite as huge as on Boxing Day but there were still 40,000 fans packed into Bramall Lane that afternoon, the vast majority baying for Wednesday blood. The *Match of the Day* cameras were also there, very rare for a Third Division game. No doubt about it this was another huge occasion.

The game started well both for me and the Blades as I caught Curran with a couple of absolute beauties. Either one would have put off many a striker, but not this lad. You could accuse him of a lot of things on a football field but being a coward wasn't one of them. He responded by whacking me on the ankle which I also took in my stride. Then he went too far by slapping my face and stamping on me behind the referee's back.

The red majority of Sheffield would have loved to see Curran sent off but I wasn't too bothered he got away with it. Kenworthy v Curran was a war and I was enjoying it. Curran wasn't getting any chance to influence the match as he had on his own patch – and we were winning. In one sweet moment just before half time, Boxing Day fortunes were reversed. Striker Barry Butlin, who'd been around the block and knew the importance of the derby, smashed a header against the Wednesday bar and the rebound ironically went straight to MacPhail. There was nothing Bolder could do this time as my mate in crime put the ball away and we were 1-0 up. As I reluctantly let Curran out of my sight to disappear into the visitors' dressing room at half time, we were even more confident of getting revenge.

As the second half started, we were reasonably comfortable without looking like killing the game off. When one goal up, you can never be certain of anything and it took one moment of brilliance from you-know-who to wreck our promising afternoon. There was no danger to our goal when Curran received the ball near our corner flag. As a defender, I was pleased to see him there with seemingly nowhere to go. But he set off on a dazzling run back towards the corner of the penalty area, leaving three or four defenders, including Sabella, in his wake. Then he let rip with a 20-yard shot that tore into the roof of the net to level the scores. Our goalkeeper swore he had an obstructed view but it was still a fine shot and one hell of a goal. Both teams huffed and puffed without finding a winner as I limped off about ten minutes from time. The final whistle went and we didn't need any reminding that the 1-1 scoreline was of far more use to the Owls, perched in the top three, than ourselves, struggling to stay in touch with the promotion pack.

There weren't many highlights during the rest of that season as we eventually limped into 12th place with a point a game from our 46 fixtures. To make things far worse, Wednesday were promoted in third spot rubbing salt into our wounds once again. We just weren't good or consistent enough. One small consolation came in the County Cup Final against Wednesday at Hillsborough. The match produced a Blades victory and a mystery I can now unravel some 30-odd years later.

I don't remember too much about the 90 minutes other than I gave Curran some personal attention and he lost his head. He was probably looking forward to a bit more freedom in a match of limited importance but hadn't reckoned on my never-say-die attitude. I gave him as much stick as in a league game and he ended up walking off the pitch.

What followed was pure farce and made good headlines in Sheffield in the next couple of months. We were presented with the decent-sized trophy, but nobody seemed to know where it was next day. Both clubs said they were looking for it amid real concern it had been stolen. What really happened was this. For a joke, I picked up the silverware, slipped it into Pedro Verde's bag and zipped it up. When he got home, he wasn't too sure what it was and put it up on his mantelpiece. The furore passed him by as his grasp of English was so poor. It was only when coach Oscar Arce went to his house that the missing trophy was discovered. The story did the rounds afterwards but I've never told anybody until now how the trophy got into Pedro's possession!

Newspapers had me all but signed on the dotted line for Leeds United during that season. It was no secret manager Jimmy Adamson was still interested in bringing Sabella to Elland Road but, when a friendly was arranged between the two clubs at Bramall Lane on a free Saturday, the papers reported Leeds had switched their attention to me. Huge transfer fees of £500,000 and £300,000 were mentioned as journalists speculated that Leeds had made a U-turn after I'd failed to get beyond the trial stage as a schoolboy and were now ready to bring me 'home'. That old Norman Hunter tag was pulled out once again as they suggested that with around 100 first team appearances under my belt I was now the real deal.

They also wrote that I'd jump at the chance to join the First Division club I watched from the terraces. Here's the truth. Yes I was very flattered to be linked with such a great club but 'home' was Bramall Lane and Sheffield United despite our struggles. Possible transfers were often ended by the potential sellers saying no and back then it would go no further. There were no agents to stir the pot and the media frenzy passed over as I stayed with the Blades. Again, I knew I was well appreciated by the supporters who voted me Player of the Year for a second successive season, the first Blade ever to achieve that honour. That was personally very satisfying after yet another disappointing campaign for the club.

Relegation, followed by a mid-table finish, meant Harry needed to pull a rabbit out of the hat to keep the board happy. His answer was to turn to a national hero when he appointed Martin Peters, goalscorer and midfield icon from England's World Cup triumph, as player-coach. Blades fans were understandably excited at the prospect of the former Tottenham Hotspur and West Ham star pulling on a red and white shirt in the Third Division. He was the player labelled '10 years ahead of his time' by England manager Sir Alf Ramsay and had became Britain's first £200,000 footballer when he signed for the Hammers. Yet Peters had many more years on the clock when he arrived at Bramall Lane and it was never going to be the same ball game in the third flight. It was no secret Harry was grooming Peters for the manager's job, so this was a very important move for the Blades.

The 'will he-won't he' Alex Sabella saga was finally settled when, after rounding off his Blades career with a goal in our South Yorkshire County Cup victory over the Owls – thought I'd mention that one again! – he was sold in the close season to Leeds United for £400,000. I've probably been a little harsh on Alex, still regarded by some Blades fans as a legend and one of the most talented players I've ever seen in a Sheffield United shirt. But we probably got the better of the deal as he didn't have the power or pace to cut it in the First Division. Irony of ironies, there was even press talk of Tony Currie, the true Blades legend Sabella never quite took the place of, coming back to the Lane with Haslam keen to do a swap deal with Queen's Park Rangers. John Matthews and I were the players reported to be in the frame to go to Loftus Road, but again the deal never materialised.

*****

Little did we know when we kicked off the 1980/81 season that it would become one of the most talked about in the history of this great football club – for all the wrong reasons. We were among the obvious promotion favourites with relegation not on our agenda at all. There were very good experienced players in our side that season. Former Manchester United and Scotland defender Stewart Houston, was in the back four alongside two full backs who rarely played together but had plenty of top flight experience – John Cutbush, who played in a Wembley FA Cup Final for Fulham, and former Norwich City star John Ryan.

We also had MacPhail and yours truly completing the defence and Peters in midfield for the first two-thirds of the campaign. There was plenty of experience up front, too, in the form of Barry Butlin, admittedly coming towards the end of his career and struggling with a back injury, and Don Givens, who arrived on loan from Birmingham City and played an unfortunate part in one of the worst days in our history.

Peters wore the famous red and white stripes for the first time in a 2-1 victory over Hull City in the Anglo Scottish Cup and scored on his league debut as we opened up with a 3-0 victory over Carlisle United at Brunton Park. We then beat Chesterfield 2-0 in a derby match at the Lane and ensured we were top of the table with a 100 per cent record after the first three games with a 1-0 home victory over Oxford United. The only blot on our copybook was losing still more bragging rights to the Owls in the first round of the League Cup.

We welcomed the chance to put the previous season's results behind us when the Sheffield rivals came out of the hat together only to find ourselves 2-0 down after the first leg at Hillsborough. We managed to get ourselves in front in the return match three days later back at the Lane but another goal by Curran enabled Wednesday to go through 3-1 on aggregate. Surprisingly perhaps that was the last time I faced the Owls in a truly competitive fixture. Defeat made it even more important we maintained our early good league form to give our loyal supporters something to hold onto.

I first crossed Peters in the very next league match, a local derby against Barnsley at Oakwell. The Tykes had genuinely good players including tough tackling defender Mick McCarthy, skilful Ronnie Glavin in midfield and another fierce competitor in striker Derek Parker. Barry Butlin flicked us in front early on before we became over-run in midfield. The final scoreline of 2-1 to Barnsley didn't tell the full story as they butchered us over the 90 minutes. Losing to local rivals was bad enough but what made it ten times worse in my book was that it looked like Barnsley wanted those points far more.

We were again letting down our supporters and I let them know I cared about what was going on by taking a few lumps out of Parker. The player/coach clearly didn't like what he saw and let me know in the dressing room afterwards. He accused me of stamping on an opponent and made it quite clear I wasn't his kind of player. I wasn't shy in telling him what I thought. 'I am not your player,' I answered, reminding him he hadn't put in a tackle all afternoon.

In a nutshell, that was why Martin Peters and Sheffield United was a marriage doomed to failure. Of course, I could see his point of view. He was a football purist used to displaying the finer skills of the game on the biggest stages. That was all well and good playing for Spurs and West Ham, traditionally good passing sides. But I defy anyone to go to Barnsley in a local derby and play that way. Tykes clashes were more like wars than football matches and the choice was put your foot in or get battered. Peters wasn't the first or the last big name to come down into the lower divisions and discover big reputations don't mean a jot. I knew the way he dealt with me at Barnsley meant my card was marked when he took over the hot seat.

Two convincing home wins, 3-0 over Swindon Town, a game in which I scored from the penalty spot just before half time and Peters also got on the scoresheet late on, and 4-2 against Blackpool meant we were still at the top of the table after seven matches with a 100 per cent home record. The latter game saw me send the Seasiders' goalkeeper the wrong way with an early penalty as we roared into a 2-0 lead inside the first 10 minutes.

Although we followed that with three successive defeats, we were still handily placed in the top six after thrashing Colchester United 3-0 at the beginning of November. I was now regarded as our penalty specialist and was quick off the mark that day, too, as we were awarded a spot kick inside the first 60 seconds. The sight of the ball soaring into the roof of the net sent us on our way with Trusson and Charles getting the others. That made it seven wins out of nine at home with only Rotherham defeating us on our own patch. Pity we were nothing like as convincing away.

With our league form becoming more inconsistent, we

trailed twice at home to struggling Carlisle. But this turned out to be a special Saturday afternoon for me as I my scored my first double in a professional match. Goal number one was a very satisfying 20 yard thump low into the net after veteran striker Bob Hatton had a shot blocked and the second was belted home from the penalty spot.

I could even have had a hat trick as I whistled a shot just wide in the closing stages as we went all out for victory. It was great, too, to score the winning goal in the first minute of extra time to see off battling Stockport County 3-2 in an FA Cup replay at Bramall Lane before we were knocked out by Chesterfield in the next round.

Our next game was laced with irony considering what was to happen on the last day. Peters didn't fancy it and left himself out of our first visit since 1893 to Fellows Park, Walsall. There was little hint of the drama to come when a fine Barry Butlin header sent us into the interval with a well deserved lead. Immediately afterwards we were awarded a penalty and my spot kick put us 2-0 in front and cruising. We then swapped goals before Walsall launched a furious late revival to get back to 3-3. Hatton's second goal sent our fans into ecstasy in the last minute only for the home side to reply straight from the kick off to clinch a very unlikely 4-4 draw. We were gutted leaving the West Midlands that Saturday evening but had no idea how vital that dropped point would prove come the end of the season.

We were eighth at Christmas with 27 points from 25 matches, still with reasonable expectations of mounting a promotion challenge in the second half of the season. Then the wheels really started to fall off. New Year started with three disappointing defeats, including a 4-0 thumping at Newport County. Our form was doing nothing for Harry's fading health and after missing the 1-0 home defeat against Gillingham, the manager decided enough was enough. He stepped down next day and Peters announced the end of his own magnificent playing career to take the job he was promised. We were 14th in the table and didn't look to be in any immediate danger with just 16 games to play. Goodness knows what Danny Bergara made of the appointment – he was the one who really deserved to be promoted.

What happened in the next four months still haunts me, as it does any Sheffield United fan of a certain age. We did beat Reading 2-0 in Peters' first home match in charge and were still 14th as late in the day as Easter Tuesday after defeating Chester by the same scoreline. But I knew all wasn't well. I may not have been a Peters' player but I was still his skipper and yet there was no relationship at all between us. In fact, that dressing down at Oakwell proved to be the only conversation I had with the boss until D-Day against Walsall on the final day of the season. Peters was guilty of double standards. Everyone knew he enjoyed a drink yet he was unhappy to see me disappearing into Victoria Wines to get myself a bottle. It was something and nothing, as far as I was concerned. I'd enjoyed myself socially for several years but wasn't breaking any club rules.

Saturday night often saw me down the Royal Oak in The Moor, a true United pub. A number of players socialised there and I chatted with fellow fans, whatever the result. It was an enjoyable part of being a footballer, albeit one today's players aren't able to share in the same way. As long as people were being reasonable, which was 99 per cent of the time, I was more than happy to discuss football with anyone. The point I'm making is that, yes, I was enjoying myself but my football wasn't suffering. I was living exactly the same way I had before Peters marched into town and doing myself justice on the field. In any case, the manager never broached that subject – or any other for that matter – directly with me.

One good example of this strangest of non-relationships between manager and captain came when he asked me over to his house at Ranmoor to collect something. I was made to stay on the doorstep as he went to look for whatever it was and handed it over to me. I just thought bollocks to the guy. He made no attempt at all to smooth things over between us for the benefit of the team. The two or three times we tried to talk in his office ended in stand-offs. I sat down and he remained standing. That made me feel he was talking down to me so I stood up myself. There was a definite atmosphere between us. He didn't fancy my playing style but whether his personal dislike was because of my popularity with the fans I will never know.

As we approached the end of that disastrous season, Peters refused to take on board the very real possibility we would get relegated. This wasn't confidence but sheer arrogance in my view. We were never in the bottom four until the last few minutes of the whole season but it was obvious to everyone we were too close to the drop zone for comfort in those last few weeks. It's a strange thing to say but relegation somehow crept up on us. We hadn't looked to be in any danger but confidence was fragile and got worse and worse as we spiralled into freefall. Suddenly we found ourselves going a goal down and thinking 'here we go again' because we weren't scoring goals at the other end.

It wasn't just the club's short term future that was becoming very confused. I was still skipper and a regular selection, apart from being left out in the defeat at Rotherham United, yet linked with a move to Peters' former club Norwich City when our destiny was on the line. The manager even went to the trouble of arranging a behind closed doors friendly with Leeds United just so the Canaries could take another look at me.

A 1-1 draw at Boothferry Park against Hull City in our penultimate match left us in 17th spot, still three places above the bottom four. But midweek results meant we needed a point against visitors and fellow strugglers Walsall on the very last afternoon to be sure of survival. Otherwise we had to rely on Swindon losing at home to mid-table Brentford. The positive side of the coin was that it was still in our hands – win or draw and it didn't matter what happened at the County Ground.

We knew though that the Saddlers would throw everything at us as only a win was enough to keep them up. Peters had no doubt we would beat them and logic was in his favour. We had a good record at Bramall Lane with 12 wins and just four defeats on home soil. Walsall had the opposite record of just four victories and 12 losses on their travels. But as anyone who has been involved in this unpredictable game knows all too well, football isn't played on paper and it was always going to be a tense afternoon.

I was well up for the battle as I got myself ready in the dressing room. Socks, boots and slip (or pants) were on when Peters told me I wasn't playing. I was shocked. Familiar faces were gobsmacked. They looked at me as if to say 'Jesus, what's happening here?' This was the most important day of the season, probably one of the most important days in the history of Sheffield United, and the skipper, a Blade through and through, wasn't going to be out there.

The manager called me into the doctor's room away from the other players to explain. 'I told you, you are leaving. I have sold you to Norwich – the deal's done!'

'No one told me,' I replied. I could have said a lot more but this was neither the time nor the place. We shouldn't have been talking about my future when the club's was at stake. Even if I was bound for Carrow Road, Peters' decision didn't make sense. Clubs often pull a player out of their side to insure against injury when a transfer is in the pipeline but I wouldn't be kicking another ball until August. It seemed like a deeply personal decision made on the hoof. Peters chose the day when our future was on a knife edge to make it clear who was in charge at Sheffield United. He proved once and for all that Tony Kenworthy wasn't his player and he did so by humiliating me in front of all my friends and colleagues. Why else did he allow me to come to the ground and even get changed before swinging the axe? Had he been certain about his line up against Walsall, he could have paid me the courtesy of telling me during the week I wasn't needed.

Peters had one more decision to make. I was our regular penalty taker so he needed an alternative. He told our midfield player John Matthews to take any spot kick. Matthews nodded but penalty taking was probably the very last thing on his mind as he took to the Bramall Lane pitch. Most players in my position would have left the ground there and then. They would have thought 'sod Sheffield United, I've had enough' and not been bothered whether we won or lost. That wasn't me. I was a fan and the most important thing in my world was that we stayed up. So I took my place in the stand and bit my fingernails with the rest of Bramall Lane. Not that there seemed too much to worry about for most of a very ordinary game. We didn't particularly look like scoring but neither did Walsall. As long as it stayed that way, we were safe.

But shortly after I switched seats to go into the dugout it all changed. Walsall were awarded a penalty and scored with about ten minutes to go. I was in shock, the crowd was in shock – now we had to pull something out of the bag. We didn't know for sure how the other game was going but last we heard Swindon were still drawing 0-0 with Brentford, a result good enough to keep them up. Then came the irony of all ironies and an incident I still go over in my mind. Unbelievably, we were awarded a penalty with time fast running out. There isn't a Sheffield United fan out there who doesn't know what happened next. Matthews didn't want to take it and instead Don Givens stepped forward. Time stood still. Could we save ourselves with almost the last kick of the season? Amid unbearable tension, the Walsall goalkeeper saved Givens' shot and the final whistle went moments later amid confusion in the home crowd.

Fans were everywhere in the minutes that followed – the pitch, tunnel, even our dressing room. Some told us we were down, others insisted Swindon had lost and we were ok after all. Best technology back then was a transistor radio and most fans passing on scores didn't even have one of those. The truth was Swindon had held on for a 0-0 draw and we were definitely down. There was desperation and raw anger about the place. I understood what was going through tortured minds because I felt it more than anyone.

When Sheffield United were relegated to the bottom division for the first and only time in our history, I wasn't the skipper and centre half but a fan. It hurt like hell when Peters told players, still in shock at what had happened, that they were to blame, not him: 'Next season you will be gone – and I will still be here,' he said. His arrogance was breathtaking. I only wish I'd knocked his block off there and then as a message from fellow Blades fans!

I haven't a clue what I did for the rest of the night. I might have drowned my sorrows or buried myself at home, I really can't say. I was numb and very confused. Going down to the Fourth Division was embarrassing, almost unthinkable. But there was another black cloud on my horizon. If what Peters said was true, I'd played my last game for the Blades. With that man in charge, there was no way back I was sure of that. I had nothing at all against Norwich City, but I was a Sheffield United player and wanted to pay back supporters who'd just suffered one of the worst days of their lives.

Fingers pointed in the direction of Matthews for refusing to take that crucial penalty – but not mine. If a player doesn't fancy taking a spot kick, better to hold your hand up and admit it. He wasn't our regular penalty taker and, when the moment came, wasn't the man for it. Did I blame Givens? Not at all. He had the guts to step up and take that all-important kick. My point was that penalty should have been taken by a man with Sheffield United running through his veins. Givens was a great professional and totally gutted at missing. But it wasn't life or death for him, just a blot on a very good career. The man who should have taken that penalty was me. The other players would have had to wrestle me to the ground to stop me doing my job.

In my head, I've taken that crucial penalty thousands and thousands of times – and never missed. However my personal afternoon had gone, I would have smashed that penalty into the back of the net and saved us. That's not arrogance, just plain fact. I had a great record from 12 yards and would have scored when it mattered most. The person I blame over that penalty – and for getting Sheffield United relegated – was Martin Peters. He won his personal battle with me but lost Blades the bloody war.

Sickening truth started to set in. A club I joined in the First Division was now in the Football League basement. I was part of a side that would go down in history for failing our fans. It was a terrible feeling and I felt guilty about having the chance to get away from it all by going on holiday to Spain. An end-of-season jolly is all well and good when you've got something to celebrate but we hadn't. We went missing at the very time our fans were taking stick because of our poor performances. Some lads let their hair down and had a good time but my head was spinning, not least because I thought I would soon be out the door.

Ryan, who played with Peters at Norwich, spoke with me in the hotel bar about the move. Because of his links with the manager, I knew he would have discussed this issue with him but felt his sentiments were genuine. He told me to keep my head up because he knew from personal experience it would be a very good move. Norwich was a very good club, he said, with very friendly folk and also a good part of the country to live. I'd also be going back up to the First Division, something that was now light years away at Sheffield United. It was some consolation, I suppose, that the manager who made my life such a misery rated me highly enough to recommend me to a top flight side. Having said that, Plan A was to stay at Bramall Lane.

Next came news that really cheered me up and blew thoughts of East Anglia clean out of the water. I was in the bar reading *The Sun* when I came across a story that Martin Peters had been sacked! Honestly, that's the way the team found out about it. We read about the managerial change in a national newspaper, there was no contact from Bramall Lane.

Word spread throughout the hotel as players and fans took the bombshell on board. There was a real buzz around the place and for me, it was the best possible development. The article didn't include any mention of a possible successor – that would come later. I had no problem raising a glass to Peters' departure because I knew it was not only good news for me but for Sheffield United as well. I've watched tapes of the guy in his prime in recent years and have no hesitation in saying he was a fantastic footballer. But it doesn't matter how good you are on the pitch as that doesn't mean you're going to be a good manager. To succeed in the hot seat you have to be a man manager and Martin Peters wasn't. His people skills, as far as I saw, were zero. I'd run through walls for some of the bosses I worked with at Bramall Lane, but could never say the same about Martin Peters.

There was still no shortage of interest in my services. Peter Anderson, now manager of Millwall, called to say he wanted to take MacPhail and me to The Den as a defensive package. Everton, Spurs and Leeds all took an interest and there was a strange approach from Forest when they were still reigning European Champions. This was too good an opportunity to miss as I wanted to meet Brian Clough. So I paid them the courtesy of going down to meet the great man and was greeted instead by his assistant, Ronnie Fenton, who merely said 'Brian wants you!' then left the room. Honestly, that's exactly what happened. I wouldn't have been bothered about Forest, however, even if they'd been world champions. The person I really wanted to meet was the new manager at Bramall Lane to find out where I stood.

It had just been announced that Ian Porterfield had switched across South Yorkshire after leading Rotherham United to promotion. We also had a new chairman in Reg Brealey who'd enjoyed success in a similar capacity at Lincoln City. Porterfield's move was exciting. He could have led the Millers into the Second Division but gave us a great vote of confidence by going down to the Fourth. It was a clever move all round. We got a young manager, oozing enthusiasm and potential, and he came to a much bigger football club for whom the only way was up.

The six million dollar question was – where did I stand in all this? Would being a Blade for years and always giving my all count against the opinion of the former manager who wanted to send me packing? I knew Porterfield would make sweeping changes but needed experienced heads to lean on. I was just itching to know what he thought. I went into that first meeting with Porterfield and Brealey ready to say my piece. Money had never bothered me but now loyalty was worth something. What, if anything, were they prepared to offer me to stay rather than seek my fortune elsewhere? I never had to open my mouth because the welcome I got from both men was a breath of fresh air. Porterfield said he really wanted me to stay at Sheffield United and that I would be an important member of the team he wanted to build. It was a culture shock to hear someone at Bramall Lane speak that way and the first time I'd felt wanted at the club for a couple of years or so.

To ensure they were backing up their words with concrete actions there was a three-year contract on the table. What a cracking deal it was for a Fourth Division footballer too. My basic wages were being increased to about £800 a week, the most I'd been paid in my career, and I also had a good signing-on fee and bonuses for appearances and for when the crowd was above 16,000. In all, it came to about £1,000 a week, more than I could spend. In addition, they provided me with a car from Gilders, completely furnished my new house at Totley, and I even had my own boot deal with Stylos. From zero to hero – I just couldn't wait to get the next phase of my Blades career started.

4

The Rollercoaster Turns

YOU MAY raise an eyebrow when I say the Blades side that won the Fourth Division title in 1981/82 was as good as any I played in. After all, I made my Blades debut in the First Division which is light years apart. That was, however, a side on a steep decline with great players from our more successful past such as Eddie Colquhoun, Alan Woodward and Ted Hemsley all on the wane through no fault of their own. The team that Ian Porterfield assembled was packed with experience, too, and proved to be a formidable unit, one which should have been kept together for longer.

The new manager did some very good business that close season, bringing in goalscoring midfielder Mickey Trusson as well as striker Steve Neville, from Exeter City, to help veteran Bob Hatton up front. Another great addition later that season was Blackpool winger Colin Morris who created and scored more than his fair share of goals. Add the fact we still had John Ryan and Paul Garner, a Blade from our First Division days, plus MacPhail and myself and we had a good solid line up playing in front of goalkeeper Keith Waugh, a great shot stopper we'd brought in from Sunderland.

Porterfield tried in vain to snatch defender Gerry Forrest from his old club Rotherham, who would have been a great signing, but topped the lot when he persuaded Hull City to sell us back Keith Edwards. It was a bad mistake, in my opinion, to allow him to slip the nest in the first place but luring him back to United shortly after netting a winning goal against us at Boothferry Park was a huge bonus for all of us. Keith may have taken stick for not working particularly hard outside the penalty area but was as good a finisher as I ever saw, scoring goals with both feet and head with equal ease.

Had he not taken the corners and given the free kicks and penalties to me, he would have ended up with a lot more than his 36 goals during that memorable season. I was very proud to be second top scorer that term with 16, including no fewer than ten from the spot. That went a long way towards making me the highest scoring defender in Sheffield United's history – a fact I'm very proud of.

Having played a number of friendlies both in Scotland and Sweden and rounded off our preparations with Group Cup games against Donny, Grimsby and Chesterfield, we were all set for kick off in front of a shirt-sleeved crowd at Bramall Lane against Hereford United. The long hard weeks of training leave you ticking off the days for the action to start for real, and we couldn't have hoped for a more encouraging start. We went ahead within 35 seconds when Steve Neville nodded home a Steve Charles corner – the first goal in the Football League that season. It got still better when John Matthews rifled home a 20-yarder inside the opening 15 minutes before we somehow allowed Hereford to get back into the game in the second half and go home with a 2-2 draw, a very disappointing outcome against a side forced to apply for re-election to the Football League at the end of the previous campaign.

The League Cup was never top of our priority list but we needed a lift when we entertained York City in a first round first leg tie in midweek. It wasn't the best of games but this was a night when both me and the Blades exorcised a few demons. Keith Waugh made a superb save from the penalty spot before we were awarded a spot kick of our own in the 66th minute. This time there was no doubt who was going to take it. The relief when my shot hit the back of the net was palpable. It was an exact reversal of what had happened against Walsall – shame Martin Peters wasn't there to see it.

My first league goal, however, came from a different kind of dead ball when I drove a shot through a fast collapsing wall at Wigan in the second league match of the season. This gave us a 1-0 victory over a side who became close rivals under the management of former Liverpool and Forest defender Larry Lloyd. The loss at Boothferry Park where Hull won 2-1 was softened by news we were in serious talks before the game to bring Edwards to Bramall Lane. He re-signed a few days later and proved to be £100,000 very well spent as he got back down to the business of scoring goals for instead of against us. Keith made his second debut in a 1-0 home victory against Scunthorpe United, a game which also saw former Forest and Stoke City midfielder Paul Richardson make his first appearance. Keith didn't have his goalscoring boots on that day, however, as it was left to me to drive in a free kick for the winner.

Winning football matches brings the same feelings of confidence and euphoria whichever division you are in. Playing well and winning most weeks became almost contagious as we went on a confidence-building early run of nine wins in ten games. Edwards got off the mark at the second time of asking with a couple of first half goals against Crewe and provided early signs that his partnership with Bob Hatton was going to be significant. Bob got a couple himself as we eventually won 4-0.

We also put four goals past York City as we visited Bootham Crescent for the second time inside a few weeks but that match was anything but easy. I got myself on the scoresheet from the penalty spot but we were 3-2 down with time fast running out. That was when Mickey Trusson turned defeat into victory with two headers, including the winner, after I surprised a few people by going on a left wing run and putting over the cross.

Our visit to Port Vale in front of the ATV Midlands cameras was a special day for Richardson, a no-nonsense midfielder. The Potteries rivalry between Vale and Stoke is well known and nobody could have been a more delighted match winner than Richo when he forced the ball into the net for the only goal. Mansfield then became another side to be hit for four, but only after they briefly silenced Bramall Lane by taking a first minute lead from a free kick. A devastating first half spell saw Edwards net a couple as we raced into a 3-1 interval lead before I rounded off the scoring from the penalty spot just before the end. That was our third four-goal haul in just five league games.

Possibly our most impressive performance of all, however, was again in front of the ITV cameras in the Yorkshire derby with Roy McFarland's Bradford City. Even the former Derby and England centre half had to admit there was only one team in it that day as we won 2-0 at Valley Parade and could have had several more. Our winning run opened up a two-point lead at the top of the Fourth Division before our sights were briefly turned elsewhere by a great League Cup draw.

The two legged tie against Arsenal, one of the First Division's best sides, highlighted our new-found spirit and belief. I had a particularly good game in the first leg in front of more than 19,000 fans at Bramall Lane where we proved we could live with the very best. Both teams had their first half moments and after the Gunners missed a chance, Keith Waugh lured David O'Leary into a headed error after a long kick downfield. Bob Hatton slotted the loose ball past the great Pat Jennings in front of the Kop to give us a 1-0 lead to take to Highbury three weeks later.

The bookies understandably rated us outsiders but we

went into the return match confident we could hang on to our lead. Scottish defender Willie Young levelled the aggregate scores with a first half header but we held out well with stubborn defending to take the tie into extra time. Alan Sunderland got the winner five minutes later but we left London convinced we matched Arsenal throughout the tie. Even Arsenal coach Don Howe sung our praises afterwards, saying if we continued to play like that, we'd quickly leave the Fourth Division behind. Porterfield wasn't complaining either – our excellent October form won him the Bells Whisky Manager of the Month award.

Promotion and title-winning campaigns would not be complete without those awful, ugly performances where you somehow dig out a good result. It happened in successive away games at Northampton Town, Torquay United and Bournemouth. The Cobblers weren't doing particularly well but were worthy of their one-goal advantage until Trusson again turned a game on its head with a much-needed double in the final frantic three minutes.

Then came two of our longest journeys of the season, both of which could easily have ended in defeats. Keith Edwards got us out of jail in the West Country after we fell behind before thousands of Blades fans, who loyally supported us all the way to Bournemouth, saw Keith Waugh make a couple of good late saves to earn us a priceless 0-0 draw.

The only blot on our landscape was a rude FA Cup shock at the hands of Altrincham, probably the best non-league side in the country. The tie looked like being a day for us to celebrate as Keith Edwards put us in front with the 100th goal of his professional career and Bob Hatton made it 2-0 with his 200th in the Football League. But, from that dominant position, we somehow allowed Alty back into the game and, with Richo having a running battle with one of their players, they somehow pulled it back to 2-2.

Our problems got worse when we went up to Cheshire

for the replay just two days later. We reshuffled our ranks due to injuries suffered in the first match and our team disintegrated still further when Mickey Trusson was sent off fairly early on. We still fancied ourselves to come through but it didn't turn out that way as we went down 3-0. That was a season, however, in which we never wasted time feeling sorry for ourselves but used our rare defeats as wake-up calls.

I was beginning to enjoy taking the dead balls. We battered Aldershot down at the Lane in early December but just couldn't score until we were awarded a free kick on the edge of their penalty area with minutes fast ticking by. What a fantastic feeling it was when I bent the ball beyond their defensive wall and into the top corner of the net to give us an overdue 1-0 lead. I nearly repeated the feat a few minutes later – Shots' goalkeeper half-saving a second free kick only for Neville to nip in and wrap up a 2-0 victory.

We were forced to dine out on that victory for a while as that match was on December 5 and we didn't manage to get back onto the pitch again until January 2 because of the terrible winter weather which felt like it would never end. The snow was relentless and we didn't have any proper training facilities available, so road runs and circuit training were the order of many a freezing day. It wasn't surprising that when we returned to action we looked a little ring rusty.

The Bramall Lane pitch was still in treacherous condition as lowly Halifax came visiting and we were relieved when Hatton gave us an early lead. We looked onto a good thing when the Shaymen conceded a spot kick and I put us 2-0 up just after the hour. Not for the first time that season, a two-goal lead proved vulnerable as Halifax hit back with two of their own and could even have ended our unbeaten home run but for a number of good saves from Keith Waugh.

Porterfield then let John Ryan go to Manchester City to take up an appointment on the coaching side and replaced him with Jeff King. The tenacious midfielder, who tormented us on Boxing Day, became one of that select band of players to make the move between the two Sheffield clubs and he proved to be a good signing.

Conditions were only marginally better when we went to Rochdale but any thoughts of whether the game should have been played were forgotten when Edwards knocked in the only goal to win us three very useful points. That was his first goal for four or five games which in that particular season was very unusual.

We then welcomed two cash-strapped sides to the Lane in Darlington and Hull City and were held to successive 0-0 draws. In my season of many penalties, I had one awarded against me in the Darlington match but that man Waugh spared my blushes by pulling off a great save. The blank against Hull produced headlines like 'Blunt Blades' and 'Blades attack off target', proof that even then the press were on your backs at the slightest hint of failure. They were writing, let's remember, about a side unbeaten in 17 league games and who hadn't lost at home all season.

Our next match against fellow promotion contenders Colchester United at Layer Road gave us a chance to show folk outside of Sheffield that the Blades were on the way back as it was a rare Fourth Division game covered by the *Match of the Day* cameras.

Unfortunately neutrals staying up to watch the highlights that Saturday evening got exactly the opposite impression and the local press gained more ammunition. We went into the clash in good spirits, particularly as we were about to be joined by an exciting winger in Colin Morris, who was tying up a £100,000 move from Blackpool. Those were difficult financial days for many clubs but the fact we were able to bring in a couple of players for six-figure sums showed we meant business. Despite that, I can honestly say we weren't at the races, even before kick off as we turned up with the wrong kit and had to borrow a strip from the home side.

It was freakish in the sense each time Colchester went forward they looked like scoring even though we did ok possession-wise. In one awful spell, the home side netted three times in just eight minutes to take a firm grip on the points. I gave us brief hope of a recovery by scoring from the penalty spot but, despite Edwards also getting himself a goal, we finished up getting well beaten 5-2.

This was a good example of how, just when you think you've cracked it, this game can kick you in the teeth. Keith Waugh was instrumental in our long unbeaten run with his fine form between the sticks but that was one 90 minutes the big man would love to forget. Such a setback could have sent shockwaves through a club still coming to terms with all we had suffered in recent years. Amazingly, that defeat left us in fourth place four points behind leaders Wigan. We were exactly halfway through the season and despite having enjoyed such a great run, weren't even filling one of the promotion places. Yet we knew we had enough ability in that team to turn things our way and that's exactly what happened.

Even better than a healthy inquest after a defeat is getting back onto the pitch as quickly as possible and putting it right. The following Tuesday saw the dressing rooms in the South Stand opened for the first time with Stockport County making first use of them. They probably wished they'd stayed there, however, as we came roaring out of the blocks to score four first half goals and banish the Colchester nightmare from our memory. Jeff King got his first goal to win over a few fans and Keith Edwards helped himself to a double. We started that night needing to win by six to move back into second spot and, but for a fine display from their goalkeeper, would have done just that.

It was same again the following Saturday when visitors York City, who ran us very close in three previous meetings, were also blown aside 4-0. Mickey Trusson set us on the way with a header and it was 3-0 by the interval with hitman Edwards getting two more. The striker's partnership with Bob Hatton was becoming virtually unstoppable as the veteran completed the scoring near the end.

Those drubbings put us briefly back on top of the table only for our performances in the following two games to earn us a good dressing down from Porterfield. It wasn't just a close range effort from Mickey Trusson that earned us a fortunate point in a 1-1 draw at Hereford, who again caused us plenty of problems after their comeback at Bramall Lane on the opening day. Keith Waugh was back to his very best in goal and the woodwork came to our aid more than once. If that was bad, our next trip to The Old Showground, where Scunthorpe hosted their biggest crowd for several seasons, was worse. Steve Neville had a shocker, coming on as a substitute for Paul Garner and getting himself sent off less than five minutes later. By that time we were 2-0 down and skidding towards defeat with my late penalty nowhere near enough to either spare us a point or the manager's justifiable anger. Sometimes you need to hear the truth and Porterfield gave it to us full barrel in the team meetings that followed. That sort of thing can either make or break you – but with the character of the lads we had in the camp there was never any doubt we would respond in the right way.

Coming back from behind to see off visitors Port Vale 2-1 was the perfect remedy. Waugh saved yet another penalty only to be beaten by the retake before a handball enabled me to step up and equalise from 12 yards, and Edwards got the winner. Two away fixtures inside three days gave us a perfect opportunity to build on that success although neither Hartlepool nor Mansfield were in any mood to make things easy for us. Our first two goals in the North East followed free kicks from Stewart Houston, another experienced head who served us well that season. Mickey Trusson scored an altogether more spectacular third to add to his impressive tally from midfield but Pool made it into a five-goal thriller and we were delighted to go home with all the points.

A mud bath of a pitch at Field Mill proved one of our toughest challenges and provided me with a moment that still torments me to this day. I'd already got myself onto the scoresheet with a close range header after my mate John MacPhail had knocked the ball back across goal. That hauled us back to 1-1 after the Stags had taken an early lead and, true to form, we went all out for a winner. When the referee pointed to the penalty spot there was little doubt in my mind what was going to happen next. As I approached the ball to face Stags goalkeeper Rod Arnold, I fully intended to drive the ball across him and into the bottom right hand corner. That's the way I took almost all my penalties and it gave me so much success. But, for a reason I can't explain, I changed my mind as I was about to take the kick and placed it unconvincingly to Arnold's left. He was a very good goalkeeper, who served Mansfield well for many years, but I made his task too easy and he made a comfortable save.

It ended a run of 13 successful penalties and was the second and final miss in my career. It still annoys me now, to be totally honest. As with the Walsall penalty when I wasn't able to do the business, I often think about placing that ball in my usual place and seeing it nestle in the back of the net. I also saw an effort cleared off the line and was walking off the pitch with very mixed feelings when Porterfield really impressed me with his attitude. Saying 'never mind' or some other platitude would have annoyed me no end because I was totally gutted at not scoring the penalty and winning us the points but instead he put his arm around me and said: 'You are as brave as a lion!' I loved that. I walked off Field Mill pushing my shoulders back.

I was also delighted with the manager's attitude after our next match which I missed due to suspension. It was a remarkable Tuesday night at Bramall Lane as we thrashed Northampton Town 7-3 to stay bang on course for promotion. But if any of the lads expected a pat on the back, they were sorely disappointed. I was in the dressing room as Porterfield let rip about the goals we conceded. We looked on course for double figures with both Edwards and Hatton getting a couple each to fire us into a 6-0 lead. Then, for no apparent reason, we suddenly conceded three quick-fire goals to change the mood at Bramall Lane before Edwards completed his hat trick to settle us back down again. There was no tea and sympathy flying around the place as Porterfield tore into the side for the way we defended. He left the lads in no doubt that, should we make the same mistakes against stronger opposition than the Cobblers, we'd get beat. In any case, we still had nothing to celebrate as we still had four points to make up on leaders Wigan.

The manager's outburst had the desired effect in the next week as we kept two crucial cleansheets. We overcame motorway delays – never ideal pre-match preparation – to win 1-0 at Blackpool on the Saturday before gaining a crucial success over title-rivals Wigan at Bramall Lane by the same scoreline the following Tuesday. I suppose your choice of man of the match in that top of the table encounter depended on whether you're a defender or an attacker. For whilst we were fighting hard to give Keith Waugh better protection after the Northampton debacle, that man Edwards was once again doing the business at the other end. The sight of our goalscorer supreme striking the ball joyously home in front of the Kop after Colin Morris crossed at full pelt probably stayed longest in the minds of the amazing crowd of 22,336 who packed into Bramall Lane. Not least because it occurred in the final seconds to leave no way back for Lloyd's men. But, for my money, our efforts at the back in keeping a genuinely good side at bay for 90 minutes plus was just as much a cause for celebration.

That attendance was an incredible statement about the loyalty of Sheffield United fans who were roaring us to success both at home and away all that season. Just why teams do so much better at home is a bit of a mystery but there's no doubt that support like we enjoyed at Bramall Lane did sometimes act as a 12th man. They'd been through a nightmare during the previous few seasons as we slid down the Football League ladder but the way they backed us so vociferously in their thousands that season made it clear we were the 'big club' on the block.

We were used to playing in front of 20,000-plus crowds but some of our visitors probably found it a culture shock. Believe me, it can take a fair bit of adjusting to if you have played the vast majority of your games in far smaller grounds. That was more likely to be the case than the idea that smaller clubs would raise their game coming to Bramall Lane. In turn we visited some very small grounds in Division Four and would often be greeted by a very strong Blades following which, at times, almost outnumbered the home fans. I think the fans found it a novelty to follow us to new and unfamiliar places.

Next up was Tranmere Rovers at Prenton Park with Blades now just a point behind Wigan with a couple of games in hand. The visit to Merseyside proved another acid test of character both for me and the rest of the team. Some players lose confidence after missing a penalty and that can get into your head. Getting back on target after missing against Mansfield Town was always going to be important but I never expected to be put on the spot twice in the same afternoon. Fortunately, I never had a split second's doubt that I could do the job. I struck both kicks low and hard in my favourite spot and both snuggled into the back of the net. The second looked as if it had saved us a point after Tranmere had led 2-1 before the home side were awarded a penalty of their own – and a great chance to win the match

– in the very last minute. Keith Waugh was beginning to get a reputation for saving penalties and did so again with a fantastic dive to his right. That draw seemed as good as a win as we trooped off at the final whistle.

Bradford City then helped to swell the Bramall Lane crowd to a remarkable 24,593 for a night match – more than European Champions Liverpool attracted to Anfield the same evening. The Bantams were also flying high, starting the match a point ahead of us in second spot. Mickey Trusson gave us visions of a vital three points when he drilled a free kick around the defensive wall but this was one match in which penalties weren't kind to us. Jeff King was penalised for a foul and there was nothing Keith Waugh could do to prevent Bradford from levelling for a hard-fought 1-1 draw. The league had by now developed into a five-horse race with Wigan, Bradford, Peterborough and Bournemouth all still in with a chance of pipping us for glory.

Bruce Rioch's Torquay, whose challenge had faded, were no match for us at Bramall Lane where three goals in a devastating six-minute spell put us on course for a crushing 4-1 victory. Then Bury manager Jim Iley helped us with our pre-match motivation by claiming their leading goalscorer Craig Madden was a better marksman than Keith Edwards, who was fast closing in on a £5,000 cash reward from Pepsi Cola for netting 35 goals. We had no doubt our Keith was in a different league but for 90 minutes at least there was nothing to split them at Bramall Lane as both scored in a 1-1 draw.

Porterfield then took the slightly unusual step of arranging for us to stay away overnight even though the trip to West Yorkshire to face Halifax Town at The Shay was one of our shorter ones. It did, however, send out the right message that the Blades meant business and that was fully reflected in our performance the following afternoon. It didn't start too well for us as Halifax took a first minute lead and had the better of the opening stages but it was all square before half time as I netted a penalty. After the break, however, there was only one team in it as deadly Edwards helped himself to another brace as we surged into a 4-1 lead before I enjoyed one of my favourite moments just before the end. Scoring a goal always leaves you feeling great – whether it was from a test of nerves from 12 yards, or a goalmouth scramble – but this had to rank as one of my best. We won a free kick 25 yards out and I struck my shot totally plumb. Had the defensive wall not collapsed, I swear it would have blown them apart. Being in front of a large contingent of Blades fans behind the goal made the moment even more memorable.

Two contrasting away performances followed, although both brought us useful points. We were very disappointing at Aldershot, where a Colin Morris equaliser was a rare highlight in a 1-1 draw, but put on one of our very best performances of the whole season at London Road to demolish promotion rivals Peterborough United 4-0. Once again, an opposition manager helped do our team talk for us as Peter Morris wasn't too complimentary about us and was left choking on his words afterwards. Edwards scored yet another double, his first taking him past Doc Pace's post war goalscoring record for the Blades.

David Webb's Bournemouth proved a far more difficult proposition back at the Lane in our second top of the table clash in just three days. We weren't too disappointed to emerge from that evening with a 0-0 draw although Edwards went agonisingly close to winning it right at the end.

With only five matches left, we were in second spot, two points clear of Posh in the crucial fourth place and three in front of Bradford City in fifth. Bury, although out of the promotion hunt, again proved very stubborn opponents at Gigg Lane. I had the agony of conceding a first half penalty allowing Madden, who also had his eyes on that £5,000 prize, to fire the Shakers in front. I swear the large following of Blades fans almost sucked the ball into the net as we piled on the pressure with time running out. Finally came the ecstasy as we got the break that earned us a vital away point. Jeff King got to the byline and Edwards proved anything Madden could do, he could do even better by eluding his marker to head home.

Having edged ourselves back to the top of the table, all stations led to Crewe, but on this occasion an almost continual stream of cars blocked main roads as Blades fans came out in their droves to cheer us on. They'd forgotten about the delays after a topsy turvy match. Crewe scored first before many of our fans had taken their places only for Edwards to bring us level before half time. Jeff King put us 2-1 up shortly afterwards yet with four minutes left it was all square again at 2-2 before King banished all thoughts of Hillsborough by bagging an important winner with his second goal of the game.

Edwards added another couple to his tally as we defeated Rochdale 3-1 in front of more than 21,000 fans at Bramall Lane to set up a chance to get over the promotion line in the return match against Posh on Saturday, May 8. Statistically we still needed a couple of points to ensure we couldn't be caught although, in reality, one was always going to be enough as we had a far better goal difference.

There was no need to worry, however, as we put the issue beyond all doubt by repeating our emphatic 4-0 victory of less than three weeks before at London Road. To make it an even more special Saturday night, I scored one of our goals. I caught the ball flush on my head just behind the penalty spot to send it soaring into the net. It was a great feeling and set us up for an exciting last week of the season with our place in the Third Division already in the bag.

We knew victory over mid-table Darlington at modest Feethams would guarantee us the title whatever happened to our nearest rivals on the final day. That was a challenge we were well up for with much of the pre-match talk focusing on how many Blades fans were going to make the trip. Darlington got the message, too, as they tried to switch the game to Ayresome Park only for the Football League to rule against it.

Nothing prepared us for what actually happened. We stayed overnight at Blackwell Grange, just off the motorway on the outskirts of the city, and were just amazed next morning at the number of coaches and cars making their way to the ground. We had to walk around the cricket pitch to get to the football area and had enough difficulty getting in ourselves, so I don't know how many fans were locked outside.

Feethams was a sea of Sheffield red and white. There were fans on top of the dugout, on the edge of the pitch, perched in trees. Today's health and safety merchants would have had a field day but it all added to a great occasion. Goodness knows how many United fans were there – like Hillsborough a few years before, the official figures were just a guideline – but we totally outnumbered the home side. There was no reason for us to worry about the officials as we had about 20 referees of our own in fancy dress! It may have been a huge match but it was also one of the easiest I've ever played in defensively as we had little problem recording a 2-0 victory. With hundreds of Blades fans already within breathing distance, the final whistle was shrouded in confusion. At one point the referee blew for a free kick then had to wait for fans to clear the pitch. Finally, he signalled the end and Keith Edwards made his way off the pitch without both boots which had been taken by celebrating fans. All good natured stuff and after publicity in the local press he got them back.

The Darlington victory meant we'd gone through the final 19 matches of the season unbeaten – winning 12 and drawing the rest – to add to the 17-game unbeaten run a little earlier. It was remarkable that our total of 96 points didn't guarantee us promotion at a canter but both the other promoted sides, Bradford City and Wigan, managed 91, enough to win most divisions. Fourth placed Bournemouth weren't that far behind on 88. Posh were fifth and Colchester, who went toe-to-toe with us for so long, ended up 24 points adrift of us in sixth.

I'll always treasure memories of that season. Porterfield restored a feeling of unity to the dressing room after the damage Peters had done and it was a great, great team to play in. The gaffer was a constant presence on the training pitch and we'd have gladly done anything for him to be successful. In contrast to United teams that followed, we had a good mix of experience and youth in that line up and it blended perfectly.

I was particularly proud of the fact we remained unbeaten all season long in front of our home fans at Bramall Lane in both league and cup. They suffered when we were relegated on our own pitch 12 months before, but stuck with us and were well rewarded. We provided them with plenty of entertainment, scoring 53 goals and conceding just 15 in our 23 home matches. Altogether we were only beaten four times in the league. Getting my hands on that medal was another personal highlight. It was the first I had won in my whole career and I was as proud of it as if we'd won the First Division itself. You'll find my medal in the Bramall Lane museum as I donated it to the club a few years ago.

Success is infectious and we were quickly looking forward to life in the Third Division with a huge surprise on the horizon during the summer. Rumours were spreading that Terry Curran, our great rival from the Sheffield derby matches a couple of years before, was on his way to Bramall Lane. He'd since been part of an Owls side that had twice faded away after being among the Second Division promotion favourites and had fallen out with manager Jack Charlton. At first, I didn't take too much notice as there's always a conveyor belt of rumours about players supposedly coming and going during the summer and most turn out to be untrue. But Blades agreed a deal with the player and the transfer fee was decided by a tribunal which understandably made big headlines in Sheffield.

I found Curran's switch strange for a number of reasons. It was hard enough for any mortal to move from one Sheffield club to the other but still harder for someone of his profile. He'd been Wednesday's top player, even having his own column in the Sheffield Star, and had not only been their outstanding performer in the matches against us but, as a natural showman, rubbed our noses in it. Coming into a fairly cosmopolitan dressing room where there weren't too many lads who'd been in Sheffield for long wasn't too much of a problem. But winning over the fans was next to impossible. Had he come from any other club, an exciting player, with top flight experience at both Derby County and Southampton would have been a great signing and given us a real boost. But this was Terry Curran of Sheffield Wednesday.

I had very mixed feelings about it after all the history between us but, once he signed and was officially a Blade, I treated him like any other team mate. You may find this surprising considering what happened between us on the pitch but Terry and I spent a fair amount of time in each other's company whilst he was at the Lane and have become life-long friends. I'm not saying we see a lot of each other nowadays but Terry's someone I can count on if I need help. You can't say that about all footballers, particularly Owls! My point is this. At heart, Terry is an Owl. He can't help it. He was born that way and will always be a Wednesday man. Yes, he made a mistake signing for United and he freely admits that now. But I can live with someone who has a passion for their football club and for the game. So, no, I wouldn't punch Terry if I saw him in the street tomorrow, but he may have to wait a while longer for that drink!

I've got no problem writing that the guy was a compulsive womaniser because if you've read his own life story *Regrets of a Football Maverick* he admits it very openly. I knew he had a girlfriend called Lorraine for one good reason – I'd been out with her before she hooked up with Terry. She was a waitress at a cocktail bar, as the Human League song goes, when she met our football crowd and I was aware that Terry and she were living together as an item. He had, however, managed to keep one pretty important secret from me and, more importantly, from Lorraine.

Anyone who knows Terry will tell you he gets an idea into his head, drops everything and goes for it. On this occasion, he decided after training he was going to watch Derby County play Manchester United at the Baseball Ground that evening. I was keen to take in an entertaining First Division fixture myself so decided to go with him. The plan was to go back to Terry's house to freshen up and change for the night ahead. But he hadn't bargained for what happened when he burst through the front door for sitting on one sofa was girlfriend Lorraine, while on the other and not looking very impressed was his wife!

I couldn't believe it. Nothing Terry had said and certainly none of his actions suggested he had a Mrs. It was clear this long suffering woman had found out about Terry and Lorraine and gone to the house to confront them. Football-crazy Terry wasn't having any of it however. He just told the shocked looking women that he couldn't cope with any of this – and they should sort it all out between them whilst he went out! So we went on our merry way to watch the Rams in action before I decided it would be best to give Terry a bit of personal space when we got back to Sheffield. By that time, the two women had thankfully been reduced to one and Terry was left to try to square things somehow with Lorraine!

Where I will part company with Terry is that I could never have done what he did and gone across the city – and, you read it here first, I actually did have my chance! Tony Toms, the Wednesday trainer, who helped me off the pitch at Bramall Lane in the Easter derby, met up with me again two or three months later at a function I was doing for the police fairly near Hillsborough. He had a word in my ear and asked me whether I'd like to play for a big club in Sheffield. I looked him in the eye and told him straight: 'I already am. I'm playing for the biggest club, Sheffield United!' Hearing that, he slapped me on the back and went on his way. He respected me for my loyalty even though I've got little doubt he'd have loved me to join him and play for Jack Charlton. Sorry, mate, you could have offered me twenty times my salary at United and I wouldn't have budged an inch. There's only ever been one Sheffield club for me.

Sheffield was bouncing back then. It was a yuppy era when plenty of young men had good jobs and cash to splash on night life and there was never a shortage of women out and about, looking for a piece of the action. I went out both with team mates and friends in the city, notably a big fellow by the name of Howard Stephenson. He was a guy with true pulling power. About 10 or 12 years older than me, I got to know Howard from my early days in the first team when he was a mate of one of the other players, David Bradford. A very keen Blades supporter, he had a good job with Abbey Life and was a socialite and Mr Fix It.

His natural habitats were the nice pubs and restaurants in Sheffield, ideal for a larger-than-life character with a big build and an even bigger appetite for the finer things in life. At first, we went out for a couple of drinks and over the months and years I found myself more and more in his company. He even turned up on our club holidays with his lovely girlfriend Gail despite our best attempts to keep at least one thing secret from him!

Maybe, because he was so often seen around the players, he wasn't always the natural cup of tea for successive managers but he did the club plenty of good turns. When the new South Stand was built, it was Howard's idea to create an executive lounge where people paid extra in return for more match day comforts. He had the contacts, knowing many professional people in and around the city, to put the whole thing together. As time went on, John MacPhail and I often went out for lunch with Howard and he became almost an unofficial agent. Whatever I wanted, he'd sort it for me, whether it was a car – or a girl! No kidding, he very rarely failed to deliver.

He got us into the best night clubs as he was very well known himself in Sheffield. Then, as I was having a drink and had time to see if any females were catching my eye, he asked if there was anyone I wished to be introduced to. He went straight over to the young lady and invited her to come to our table for a drink with Tony Kenworthy. Around 95 per cent of the time they said yes, so whilst most of my friends were dancing and enjoying the music, I was chatting up a good looking woman. Very rarely did I have any problem afterwards. Naturally, there would be a few occasions which got a bit hairy when we were out with our girlfriends – as we tended to do as a team every month or so – and could easily bump into someone I'd slept with. But, again, they tended to behave themselves very well in those days. Usually they kept their distance if they saw I was with someone. There was a social etiquette in those days which worked well.

The phone was passed to me at Bramall Lane one morning with the message a young woman was on the line. Sounded interesting. 'I just wanted to tell you I really enjoyed Saturday evening,' she said. 'Thanks very much for taking me out.'

'I'm sorry,' I replied. 'That wasn't me. I wasn't there on Saturday ...'

'But he told me he was Tony Kenworthy,' she went on. Now, the mystery was revealed. Some quick-thinking opportunist had chatted her up with the help of pretending to be a Sheffield United footballer! Anyway, she sounded very nice, so I took my chance and invited her out for a drink.

I also had a semi stalker at Bramall Lane. It started when this girl was about 15 or 16 years old. She turned up at the ground almost every Friday, telling me she was a keen Blades fan and asking me to autograph this and that for her. At first, I didn't take much notice. But, as the weeks and months went by, I began to wonder just how many copies of my autograph she wanted. Some of the items she asked me to sign were amazing, to be honest. I was always as polite as possible and certainly didn't do anything to encourage her romantically. Trouble was her mother wasn't helping any. She often turned up with her daughter but never said anything to divert her daughter from what was fast becoming an unhealthy obsession. She turned up as regular as clockwork and it got to the stage where I deliberately drove to the ground early on a Friday to try to avoid her. She must have got hundreds of my autographs and it was beginning to get more worrying as she put the odd note on my car, saying how much she loved me. Then I'd turn on the radio and find yet another request dedicated to me by the same young woman. She was on my case for several years, yet we never had what I would call a proper conversation, let alone go out. We've all read of cases when such attachments have got out of hand, so I was lucky.

I wasn't married during that hectic social time although I did have a lovely live-in girlfriend called Michelle for five years from 1983 to 1988. She was an attractive young woman with a good career of her own. When we met, she was working for a cosmetics company called Revlon and already bringing in reasonable money. She then rose up through the ranks as we lived together at Whirlow Cottage to become area manager. I was away from home through my football and she was often away through her work. With the best will in the world, it becomes very difficult to hold any relationship together – however good it may be – when you're not spending much time in each other's company.

The distance between us became wider as I took advantage of Michelle being away to go out on the town and enjoy myself. I didn't mean to hurt her but that's the truth. I'm just being honest and reflecting that our relationship, in the end, was just not meant to be. The Blades, like most other football clubs, preferred their players to be married or have a steady long-term partner. To put it bluntly, this meant they had a better chance of knowing where we were and what we were doing when we weren't playing. Footballers with young families, in particular, were far less likely to go out drinking or pulling girls. I suppose this just shows that, in my particular case, I had my cake and ate it. For I was one of the lads who did have a girlfriend and did all the things they expected of the players who were single.

Before anyone gets tempted to get on their high horse, just think about this for a moment. You're fit, reasonably good looking, and have a few quid in your pocket. Girls, stunning girls at that, recognise you instantly, want to have a drink with you and are literally throwing themselves at you sexually. What would you do given the same circumstances? I'm sure every red blooded man would agree it takes a very strong willed individual to keep your distance – a far stronger person than me, that's for sure. I'm not arguing what I did was always right. In an ideal world, it wouldn't have happened. But it was mostly just good fun between young people with similar desires. Women have always been attracted to footballers and always will be. That's the way of the world. They knew what they wanted in my day and, equally, knew what we had to offer.

Most of the lads I played with at Sheffield United had wives or regular girlfriends and the girls knew the score. They weren't after long term relationships or a quick kiss-and-tell to sell to the Sunday newspapers who wouldn't have paid for their silly stories back then anyway. They wanted a damned good night out and, hopefully for us, a happy ending! Once the evening was over, both sides knew we'd probably not see each other again. Neither of us got hurt, we were just doing what young people do when the opportunity presents itself.

Not all my team mates saw things the same way, but we all enjoyed a good social time nevertheless. Take two of my defensive partners, John MacPhail and Paul Stancliffe. Great players on the field, complete opposites off it. Socially, they were chalk and cheese. MacPhail was unattached, a good looking lad and loved the company of women. Like me, he was rarely short of female attention. Paul, on the other hand, was one of the most devoted family men I have ever come across. He would never cheat on his wife and I certainly didn't see him make a move on another woman. That was his way and I totally respected and admired him for it. But even if we were different animals, we would always share a drink and enjoy ourselves.

To say there was no comeback for our behaviour wasn't quite true. There have always been folk who contact football clubs to report players who they've seen out on the town. And that happened frequently enough in the 1970s and 80s. I'd get called into the office every now and again and told I'd been seen at this or that pub or night club before a big game. Usually, it was a load of rubbish as I played by the club rules. We weren't allowed to go out on a Thursday or Friday night before a match on a Saturday and I respected that. I chose where and when I went out carefully and didn't let it affect my performances or the likely results of my team.

*****

Other than Terry, we didn't make too many changes to our line up for our first season back in the Third Division although Barnsley midfielder Ray McHale joined us and Bob Atkins, a defender-cum-midfielder, forced his way into the side on occasions. Veteran Bob Hatton continued to partner goal machine Keith Edwards for most of the season until we brought in another striker with pedigree and experience in former Leicester City player Alan Young. This could so easily have been the perfect partnership with Youngy knocking defenders about and Edwards banging in the goals, had the Scot been the same physical animal he was at Filbert Street when I had the difficult task of playing against him on a number of occasions.

Youngy was and is a terrific bloke who became one of my genuine mates during his spell at Bramall Lane. I liked him because he was the type to give me some banter back in the dressing room and not, as some of the lads thought, because he had a very good looking girlfriend in Karen. The four of us did, however, spend a lot of time together off-the-field where Alan enjoyed having a drink and letting his hair down a little. He played hard on the pitch and off it and was therefore my kind of person.

The problem was he never got the opportunity to show Sheffield United fans how good he was because, having always been a player who put his body on the line, he was beginning to count the cost. He suffered a number of bad injuries to his back and legs before he joined the Blades but almost came to grief with us in very strange circumstances. An opponent stamped on his hand during a match at Bramall Lane, causing the web between his fingers to split and his hand to blow up like a balloon. There were genuine fears for a while that he'd lose his hand altogether but, thankfully, it never came to that. I missed Youngy a lot when he moved on and I'm sorry to hear that he's suffered from his fair share of demons since the end of his playing career. It was great, however, to hear his unmissable voice on the phone as I was completing this book, telling me he has also written his own autobiography. He has found a niche doing summaries for Radio Leicester and remains a popular figure with many Leicester City supporters who remember him at his best.

Ambition at the club was clear, but the 1982/83 season never really caught fire. We kicked off with a 4-1 defeat at Pompey, being reduced to ten men when long-serving Paul Garner became one of the first victims of the newly introduced rule of sending players off for deliberate handball. We managed to maintain our Bramall Lane fortress during the first few weeks with victories in our first four matches in front of our home fans, including a 3-1 League Cup success over Hull that proved enough to take us through to the second round after two legs. Then Gillingham became the first side to defeat us on home soil since Walsall some 17 months earlier when they won 2-0, our third reverse on the spin.

It was up and down as we smashed eight goals past Grimsby Town in another two legged League Cup tie but failed to find any consistency in the league. By this time the rumours surrounding Curran were of a different kind and just before Christmas he went off to First Division giants Everton for a month's loan. This was a sign that the controversial move wasn't proving a success either for the player or the club. Bramall Lane fans certainly hadn't forgiven him for being Wednesday's talisman and were giving him a hard time. It still seemed strange, however, that after going to the trouble they did to sign the player, the club were willing to loan him out just three or four months later.

During the time when Curran was missing we completed a cup double over Hull City, beating them 2-0 after a replay in the FA Cup, to set up a tasty third round tie against First Division Stoke City. We drew 0-0 at Bramall Lane before going down 3-2 in an exciting replay at the Victoria Ground during which Curran produced perhaps his best performance in a Blades shirt. It didn't, however, help us too much that he was back at Bramall Lane for the rest of the season after talks with Everton over a permanent deal had broken down. To be fair, I don't think Terry wanted to be at Sheffield United and that had an influence on the pitch.

We did have one bright spell at the beginning of March when we followed up a couple of Bramall Lane victories with success at Millwall and revenge over the Gills only for my season to suffer a real setback in our next home match against Oxford United. Ironically, my injury was suffered during a moment of triumph. The ball was flicked on from a corner for me at the far post to volley into the net for the decisive goal in a 3-2 victory. But I came off the pitch that day knowing something was wrong. The moment I struck the ball I felt my ankle go twang, like an elastic band. It swelled up afterwards to give me more concern and was the start of ankle problems that haunt me to this day.

Nobody at United could get to the bottom of my problem. The treatment I received was fairly minimal – some ultrasound, heat lamp, ice, that type of thing – but I was soon needing cortisone injections to mask the pain and ensure I got through the season which ended with us in a respectable, if unspectacular, 11th place. For the second year running, our home form was really good with 16 wins at Bramall Lane. The problem was we lost just as many on the road.

The other significant development was the end of my centre back partnership with John MacPhail who was loaned to York City in February. We spent so much time together we were more like brothers but despite being close friends, I can say with total honesty he was one of the top Sheffield United defenders. At one stage, I genuinely think he could have got a full international cap for Scotland. Manager Jock Stein came to watch him in a match at St Mirren but chose the wrong game. John didn't have much choice in his eventual move – the club told him they wanted to do the deal. I remember thinking there was no way the Blades could find a replacement half as good as John MacPhail but Porterfield proved me wrong with Paul Stancliffe, who played for him at Rotherham and went on to do a great job for us.

5

Injury Time Down the Lane

IT WAS a major personal disappointment that my last three seasons at Bramall Lane, a successful period when we regained our Second Division status and showed ambition to go still further, were so badly hit by injury.

I ignored cuts and bruises, even stitches, and got on with the game. I played with broken bones when I could, even though I didn't always know it at the time. Going back, one of my most serious injuries occurred when I was still a teenager trying to establish myself in the Blades side. It didn't put me out of the team and was never properly diagnosed or acted upon, but it causes me absolute agony to this day. It happened, as with most of my bad injuries, in a completely innocent collision. I played by the sword and lived by it, but sometimes things happen that nobody can do anything about. It was during an Anglo-Scottish cup tie against Dundee at Bramall Lane when I was in the opposition's penalty area trying to challenge for a high ball. Their goalkeeper came out with no other intention than to clear the danger by getting to the cross first. But he came out with his knees up and kicked me in the small of the back as he claimed possession. I was in pain but had no idea what had happened. In fact, the goalkeeper had just crushed my vertebrae, in effect breaking my back.

I was in some discomfort but the club's medical team were none the wiser. It was only when our striker Barry Butlin said I ought to go and see a doctor privately near Nottingham that I got nearer to the truth. That painful visit became something I did four or five times a season. I drove over there and he produced a needle. First time he did it, I almost panicked wondering where on earth it was going to go. He told me not to move an inch, which wasn't easy, and gave me an epidural in my spine. Afterwards I'd lay in traction for the night before getting up next day and driving back to Sheffield.

There was a touch of comedy about it. I was approaching the doctor's place one day when I spotted two good-looking girls coming the opposite way. Here I was a young man almost bent double walking along, so I pretended to pick something out of my sock to ease my embarrassment. I went into the doctor's surgery to tell him I was tilting to one side only for him to suggest tilting to the other! Yet the wreck he saw before him would be playing professional football two or three days later when the adrenalin kicked in and I'd forgotten all about the pain. I played with that injury for the rest of my career. I found out years later an operation could fuse the vertebrae back together. But my body was so battered and had been put under the knife for so many serious operations, I decided that, if humanly bearable, I'd take the pain and leave well alone.

Fans question your eyesight when you miss an easy chance but playing with one of my eyes closed was another occupational hazard. There were many times when I could and probably should have held up my hand and told the manager I was injured. But it wasn't something players did easily. If you were in the team you wanted to stay there, and being injured put that in jeopardy. So I took a jab or a few stitches, patched myself up, and the excitement of being out there on the pitch usually got me through.

One good example of the way things were came in a game against West Ham United at Upton Park. I went into a tackle with Frank Lampard, father of the Chelsea and England star, and my knee split wide open. I was taken off the pitch and treated by the home side's physio who put in several stitches without any injection and told me to get back out there. If it happened again, he'd stitch me back up at the end. These days I'd have been taken off and not played for weeks and rightly so. But I made it through to the final whistle that night and was playing again at the weekend.

Talking of injections, cortisone must have been invented just for me. It was regarded as a miracle cure. It didn't matter too much what the injury was, just reach for the needle and it would do the job. To be honest, I was suffering from a bad case of white coat syndrome. Whatever someone told me about a medical condition, I believed it as long as he or she was wearing a white coat. Almost all of us did. Who was I to argue? There was no discussion of the potential longer term consequences of masking over the pain and putting a bad injury at further risk. I'm not criticising anyone here because the medics told us what they knew at the time, which turns out now to be not a lot. Everything was done 'for the moment'. Those were the days of club power as opposed to player power today, when the club regarded you as their property. They urged me to do whatever I could to declare myself fit and, in my naivety, I thought that was always best for me. I have no idea how many cortisone injections I had during my career – it happened so often, I didn't have time to count.

The period I'm generally referring to here, however, was later in my career and began when I had a very delicate operation on my left ankle during the summer before the 1983/84 season. I'd like to dedicate this chapter, if that's possible, to surgeon Neville Kaye, who performed that operation and several others in following years. Neville was

Sheffield United's club surgeon who almost single-handedly kept me on a football field. Words like 'hero' and 'legend' get banded about like confetti when there are genuine good folk in the background doing far more important jobs with livelihoods in their expert hands. I'm convinced even the manager and officials at Sheffield United had no idea how responsible Neville was for putting me back together and allowing me to make a series of comebacks. They just let players get on with it when they got injured.

Football has changed – not all for the better, I might add – but when it comes to injuries, training, rehabilitation and generally looking after players, we're now light years ahead of where we were. Hopefully that will save a lot of today's footballers from a repeat of my pain when they get to their 50s.

Allow me to introduce you to another leading character in my injury story. Jim Dixon's main virtues were that he was a very impressive athlete and a personal friend of Blades manager, Ian Porterfield. Managers always tend to take people they like and trust to their various clubs, so Porterfield employed Dixon as our trainer when he came to Bramall Lane after the pair worked together at Rotherham United.

Jim's idea of training was a five-mile trip around Gray's Park in Sheffield. Now I never shirked hard work but, for most of my career, I didn't particularly enjoy running. If I had, I might have trained to be a marathon runner rather than a footballer. Instead we should have seen a football a lot more during our preparation for matches. After all, it's what you do with a ball that determines whether you're successful on a Saturday. I'll put my hands up and admit I was one of the chief moaners and groaners when we went for yet another long run. No better or worse than most of my team mates physically, I'd usually finish in the middle of the pack, totally shattered and none the wiser why we'd all been put through such agony.

Had the long runs been my only complaint about Dixon that wouldn't have been too bad, but, when given the job as club physio he was beyond a joke. He wasn't medically qualified and hadn't got a clue. In all honesty, they may as well have given the job to an office clerk or a factory worker. If one of the United players had an injury he barely knew where to look, let alone what to do. 'Put ice on it,' was about the sum of his medical knowledge. Thanks a lot, mate, I knew that much myself.

When Jim couldn't fix it, which was 99 per cent of the time, we got referred to the club doctor whose answer for everything was to hand out pills. The most useful thing he did at Bramall Lane was help the players out if we caught anything nasty from our sexual adventures off the field. Then he gave us a few tablets and they would work a treat. Anything else and he wasn't quite so on the ball, so to speak.

Getting real injuries was a very common thing for me as a defender. It won't surprise you to hear me say football is a game for forwards. Many times at Bramall Lane, our leading goalscorer, Keith Edwards, would be neatly blow-dried and chatting merrily to the local media after a game whilst I was still nursing my battle wounds in the bath. 'Well, I scored the winning goal today,' he'd tell me and I couldn't argue. But there's a big difference in my book between a striker and a defender's lot. When the ball bounces in the penalty area, a forward thinks whether to put his head in among the boots and bodies to get a decisive touch. A defender has no choice. Fans forgive the odd bad pass or tackle here and there, but if a defender ducks out of a challenge and costs his side a goal they're on his back and rightly so.

It became obvious that the injury I received against Oxford United wasn't going to go away. Eventually I got the message something was wrong and needed checking out. There was no point asking either marathon man or the doc, so I went straight to the specialist. There was no such thing as scans in those days, of course, so Neville listened to what I had to say, took a quick look, and told me the only way he could find out the extent of the injury was to open me up. So I went into Claremont Hospital in Sheffield and Neville did the business.

When I came round, he told me the news. My inside ankle ligament had been hanging by a thread, ready to snap and cause still more damage at any moment. It could easily have been a career-threatening injury. Neville used his skills to re-attach the ligament and clean it all up and get rid of the floating bone. I still didn't have too much idea how bad it actually was until the strapping and bandages were removed. There I was with stitches from my left toe all the way up to my shin. 'This could be a problem,' Neville told me. To be fair, he had a good point.

It never crossed my mind my playing career could be over. My only thought was to get fit and back playing as soon as possible. In fact it took several months before I was able to regain my place in the Blades first team, months that taught me a lot about myself and the way football worked.

I'm not having a go at Porterfield here as most managers both at Sheffield United and elsewhere were much the same. If you were in the first team the boss would talk to you, involve you in things, and when things were going well on the field, you could even be flavour of the month. If you weren't in the first team, however, you were very much on the outside – all the more so if you happened to be injured. I had never been out for an extended time before so had no idea what an impact it would have on my Saturday afternoons and the rest of my life. I can only describe it as soul destroying. Even though I'd been in the manager's plans and thoughts before the injury, afterwards I was treated like a leper. It seemed the whole of the football world was passing me by and I was left on my own to get on with it.

Dixon would never have got me past first base in my rehabilitation, and unless I was getting lucky with the wrong kind of girl, doc wasn't going to be much use either. So I went to the gym and worked by myself. I missed the chat and banter of the lads doing their training in the morning, and when it was time for them to take the afternoon off, I'd be back in the gym on my own yet again. None of the management team came to ask me how I was getting on. I may as well have been in a parallel universe.

Saturdays were the best of a bad lot, particularly if the first team was at Bramall Lane. I hear a lot of footballers saying they don't like watching, but I went because at heart, I'm a supporter. If I hadn't been a Sheffield United player during those days, I'd have been standing on the Kop roaring the lads on. So I watched United's home games and usually the reserves or the youth team when we were away.

I couldn't wait to get back into the side and was thrilled when I took my place for the visit of Wigan Athletic at the end of September 1983. Better still I marked the occasion by getting a goal with a far post header to help us earn a point from a 2-2 draw. It had been a long hard haul to get back and the last thing on my mind was that history was just about to repeat itself all over again. Yet, after just three or four first team matches, I realised I may still have a problem. My ankle was flaring up again during training and all the 'physio' could say was heap more and more ice on it.

Nobody at the club was either equipped or willing to look into it any deeper than that. So I went back to Neville to seek his more expert opinion. Again, he had little option but to put me under the knife at Claremont to see what was happening. So he opened up the side of the ankle and I was left with another huge scar. All the ligament sheets were dry having caused friction and swelling. The great man did a major job re-attaching the ligaments again and cleaning them out but it was a real mess. It looked like he had stitched another foot on. Afterwards Neville looked me in the eye and said: 'If I was you, I'd buy myself a pub!' Those were his exact words. He meant well but the thought didn't cheer me up – my mate Howard did that by bringing a few girls into hospital to keep me occupied for an hour or two.

I considered Neville's comment but came to a different conclusion. I still wanted to give it a real go. We were coming towards the end of the season and I never had any contact from the Blades – no phone call or anything to ask how I was. With nobody at the club working with me or able to offer anything more than token treatment, I became a regular visitor at Neville Kaye's house just off Ecclesall Road, even when I didn't have an appointment. The way he dealt with me was really truly remarkable.

He was busy to the point of being rushed off his feet yet never once turned me away. He politely asked me a couple of times to wait whilst he dealt with something else but never kept me for long. Without any other expert guidance, I would keep on asking him whether it was ok for me to go for a run or step up my fitness routine and he checked on my progress and offered his advice. When he finally said I could go for a run, I was thrilled – and that comes from someone who didn't enjoy running. Given the green light, I pounded the streets of Sheffield like never before and, after about a month, found I was actually enjoying and looking forward to it every day. It's a well-known fact that endorphins kick in and you can get a real kick from running but this was the first time it had happened to me. I wasn't eating very much, so I soon got trim and fit.

When I got back to training with the lads and going for our five-mile trek around Graves Park, Steve Charles was still the frontrunner but, to the great surprise of Dixon and co, I was no longer in the pack but in second place, only about 50 yards behind. The management could scarcely miss the fact I was in very good shape. More importantly, my ankle was looking better too. I went to see Neville to check how it was doing. He flexed it and said that, as long as I continued to look after myself, it should be fine for me to play again. He did warn me though that the injury would catch up with me again in later life, not that he expected me to take much notice.

One person who really showed his true colours and was one of the few to offer me real support during that difficult time was Keith Edwards. That may surprise a lot of folk because the image surrounding the bloke was typical of many goalscorers – arrogant, lazy and a bit selfish. Well, I'll tell you this, I didn't have any complaints about Keith on the field where he was one of the greatest goalscorers in our history. Strikers can sometimes appear lazy, particularly those who are very single minded in doing what is probably the hardest job in the game – putting the ball into the back of the net. Off the field, I'd known Keith from our early days at Bramall Lane and considered him a man's man. He enjoyed a bet and a game of snooker just like many of the fans who followed him every Saturday. I discovered more about the real Keith Edwards when, thanks to the chairman Reg Brealey, I went to Woodhall Spa for three or four days training during my rehabilitation. Keith came to see me and told me I was still limping when I thought I was ok. When management and most colleagues were turning a blind eye to my progress, Keith offered to come training with me during his afternoons off to give me some company. Nothing arrogant or selfish about that attitude and I appreciated his help a great deal.

Although I missed the majority of the campaign on the pitch, I had plenty to enjoy as a fan as, led by Edwards having one of his prolific seasons, we stayed in and around the promotion zone. I never missed a game at Bramall Lane where we were particularly strong and kept in close touch with our away matches, usually through the 15-second reports every few minutes or so on Radio Sheffield.

There was no shortage of action either for the fans to enjoy as we scored five each against Scunthorpe United, Southend United and Bolton Wanderers and one better in a 6-3 thriller against Orient. With just a few games to go, we were in a very good position to clinch one of the top three spots only to face the strange challenge of playing one of our main rivals, Hull City, in the area final of the Associate Members Cup. A Boothferry Park crowd of less than 4,000 told the story that even the prospect of a Wembley final was small fry compared with getting back into the Second Division. The Tigers won the tie 1-0 but we had the last and more significant laugh a few weeks later.

There were last gasp nerves as we were beaten 2-1 at home by Wimbledon and then Bolton gained revenge with a 3-1 success at Burnden Park in our penultimate match. Even a 2-0 victory over Newport County in our last game at Bramall Lane wasn't quite enough to book the champagne as Hull City still had one last chance to overhaul us on the Tuesday night at mid-table Burnley. They faced the difficult but not impossible task of winning by three clear goals to leap above us into the third promotion slot behind the Wombles and champions Oxford United.

That was a very memorable night as I joined several members of the Blades squad in a pub down The Moor to listen nervously to the local radio commentary. The tension was almost unbearable as Hull quickly found themselves two goals to the good against a team with just pride to play for. As our winger Colin Morris who was at Turf Moor told us later, most folk would have put their mortgage on Hull's star forward Brian Marwood clinching victory and promotion instead of lifting a gilt edged chance towards the end over the bar. The divide between success and relative failure really was that close. Over 46 hard fought league games, the two sides finished level on 83 points but we were the ones celebrating promotion. That made for a very good night down the pub!

I had mixed feelings; it was very disappointing and unusual for me to play such a small part in our season but, as a supporter, I was thrilled we took another major step on what I hoped would be a journey all the way back to the First Division. My season wasn't quite over, however, at least in the eyes of the manager and his crazy physio. An unexpected problem arose as the Blades were preparing for a close season tour abroad. The thought of some team bonding and socialising with a couple of friendly games thrown in was a nice one after all I'd been through. Trust that man Dixon to ruin it. 'The boss wants you to play in a reserve game at Liverpool,' he told me. I replied that, although I was training well, the ankle was still sore and I wasn't really ready. I knew also that the game was a completely meaningless end-of-season affair – even less cause to put my ankle at risk.

For some reason, management wouldn't let the issue drop. I was called into the office to see Porterfeld who went through the routine of asking the doc for his view. I was ready to play, so was there any problem? Doc responded to the loaded question by saying he couldn't see how it could do any harm. When I stuck to my guns, Porterfield was furious and stormed: 'Right, if you don't play at Liverpool, you're not going with us on tour. I won't take you unless you're ready to play.' The door virtually came off its hinges as I took my leave!

The tour wasn't the be-all and end-all as far as I was concerned. I was looking forward to the trip but had Porterfield left me out because I wasn't match fit I'd have accepted it. What really made me angry, however, was he took his mate Paul Stancliffe who'd also been injured and never got onto the field. To be fair, the boss wasn't having the best of times at home with his wife and his judgement may have been clouded by Dixon. To me, however, it highlighted how my whole injury issue was handled. Club surgeon Neville Kaye was the only person medically qualified to have a worthwhile opinion, all the more so as his handiwork had saved my career. Also, I was the one who knew how the injury felt. After two lengthy spells out of the game, I knew I needed a couple more weeks before putting my recovery to the test. It was so frustrating the club took such a firm stance and didn't trust my opinion after all I'd done for the Blades over the years.

Meanwhile interesting things were happening back on the field. The club was literally buzzing with anticipation about the new kick-off back in the Second Division for the 1984/85 season. Clearly the manager had no intention of resting on his laurels after seeing us gain two quickfire promotions under his leadership. Getting back into the second flight saw him bring some very big names into the club – with gasps of admiration from the terraces but not necessarily in the dressing room.

Our defence was stiffened by the additions of Liverpool legend Phil Thompson who arrived that season along with Ray Lewington, Mel Eves and former Villa skipper Dennis Mortimer. Two more big Villa names who joined us during that era were Peter Withe, scorer of the winning goal in the 1981 European Cup final, and Ken McNaught, another defender with significant pedigree. I didn't have any problem with any of the signings myself, finding Thompson, in particular, to be a fantastic fellow to have around the place, but new boys coming in on higher wages than many others in the squad were bound to cause a few problems.

This was a significant change of policy from Porterfield and in my view not a good one. After tasting success with a young side who formed a very close knit dressing room, the chairman had given the green light for the manager to spend a few bob and see if we could go all the way into the top flight. Had the players we signed been in or around their prime, it may have worked a treat. Instead they were almost all towards the end of their playing careers and, through no fault of their own, were never going to give us the boost we hoped for.

This was the point where I felt Porterfield was losing his way through listening to people around him, including Dixon, who didn't know that much about the game. Strangely, the big names weren't always treated that well. I couldn't understand why the manager insisted on Thompson, who'd been there and done everything in the game, travelling long distances to several away matches and then being left out of the 12. It wasn't very respectful to a player of his status and sent out confused messages to the rest of us.

*****

It was a major personal boost to be fit and raring to go at the start of that season and, putting my battle scars to one side, I was optimistic once again. I was still only 26 years of age, with plenty of potential miles still on my football clock, and the Blades were within one more promotion of getting back into the top flight. My ambition to play First Division football again drove me into the new season, and the surgeon's words into the back of my head. Following the pre-season tour of Sweden, I got myself into the side in my favourite centre half position for the rest of the friendlies.

After being named as substitute for the opening day 2-2 draw at Wolves, I had a good run in the side during the first third of the campaign. Disappointingly, however, we weren't hitting top gear as a team with promising victories over Cardiff City 2-1, and Notts County 3-0 at Bramall Lane being our sole successes in our first 10, Division Two games.

We also got a League Cup hiding against mighty Everton after holding them to a 2-2 draw on home soil. The return game saw me given a first hand insight into just how good Adrian Heath and Graeme Sharp were as we went crashing out by 4-0.

I was out of the side again for two or three months after another heavy defeat against Middlesbrough before, having got myself fit and ready for first team action, Porterfield sprung a surprise by asking whether I wanted to go and have a chat with Swansea City boss Colin Appleton.

It was a Friday night and they were playing a few miles up the road at Barnsley so I didn't have anything to lose. I went there with no pre-conceived plans of uprooting and going to Wales but Appleton took the initiative. He kept asking what I wanted and answered positively to all my demands. With no sign of Porterfield selecting me for the first team, I was genuinely interested in the offer before events took another unexpected turn. Porterfield called me in for a chat and told me to forget about the move to Swansea because he was putting me back in the side on the Tuesday night. That made all the difference to me.

The manager restored me to the side at left back, a move which coincided with some better defensive performances from the Blades. We held Notts County to a 0-0 draw in the return game at Meadow Lane before keeping two more welcome clean-sheets as a goal in each game from Keith Edwards helped us to win 2-0 at Grimsby and see off Oldham Athletic by the same scoreline at Bramall Lane. I also contributed to a 0-0 draw in a friendly against IFK Gothenburg in Sweden before we became badly unstuck at one of the most hostile grounds in the country. You couldn't pack more than a few thousand into unhomely Plough Lane but the Crazy Gang fervour, plus a small difficult pitch and an unforgiving home crowd, always made it one of the most difficult of places to play at. We were beaten 5-0 that day to undo much of our good work.

I was looking forward to Leeds United's visit to Bramall Lane and delighted when I was named in the number three shirt. That was still a very big occasion for my family with Mum and Dad coming to support me, but this day was to turn into a disaster. There was bitter irony as the incident that caused me another serious injury setback involved former team mate Gary Hamson. It was a complete accident, although it may well have resulted in Gary being shown a red card today. I went to clear the ball and Gary put his foot up in a genuine attempt to block. Instead he caught me flush on my knee cap and knocked it clean off. It actually moved about six inches and ended up in my thigh. I was collapsed in a heap when Dixon told me to get up! I'll just run that one past you again: I'd been knee-capped and the physio wanted me to get back on my feet and carry on playing. Unbelievable, but true!

Next thing I knew I was back in the dressing room with Neville Kaye looking over me. Luckily for me, he'd been watching in the stand and rushed down straightaway. He got everything organised for me to go to the Hallamshire Hospital in Sheffield for surgery and we were waiting for the ambulance. So off I went in my kit and my knee was operated on barely an hour after the injury happened. How's that for service? Coming round from the anaesthetic, first face I saw was Billy McEwan, one of the coaches down at the Lane. We hadn't exactly seen eye-to-eye but my opinion changed that day. He took the time and effort to be there when I woke up from my nightmare to find out exactly how I was. Phil Thompson was another hospital visitor, telling me he'd never seen an injury like it.

You struggle to find words to describe your feelings when lightning strikes for a third time. It was obvious I was going to be out for another extended spell and I remember thinking 'Jesus, am I really going to go through all this again?' Neville offered more friendly advice. 'Haven't you had enough, Tony?' he said. 'You've been here so many times.'

My parents asked whether it was worth all the hassle trying to get back on the field again and my girlfriend was of much the same opinion. They knew what a battering my mind and body had already taken within such a short space of time and how difficult it had been to keep going. They all wanted the very best for me and, in Neville's case, you can understand his frustration at having to continually piece me back together. But there was no danger of me giving up the game just then. Football was all I'd ever known or wanted and I couldn't wait to prove them wrong all over again.

I knew it would be a lonely road back and it was once again a case of strong will and tunnel vision kicking in. I deliberately forgot all the negatives from Neville and well meaning friends and relatives and dedicated myself to getting fit and well. Today I'd probably be surrounded by medics helping me every inch of the way and be sent off to America or some other far-flung location to help with my recovery. Instead I was left again to my own devices and began to pound the Sheffield streets once back on my feet.

I was back in contention for a place for the beginning of the 1985/86 season which was to prove my last at Bramall Lane. I played in the pre-season matches, getting myself a goal against Newcastle United and doing enough to be selected as full back in the opening league match of the season, a 3-0 victory over visitors Stoke City. In all, I played the first 10 matches in the number three shirt as we helped ourselves to eight goals over the two legs in the League Cup against Rotherham and made a promising start in the league.

I was then out of the side until around Christmas when I forced myself back into Porterfield's line-up for my last eight matches in a Blades shirt. I didn't know it was going to be the case at the time but my last league appearance at

Bramall Lane was again at full back in a 1-0 victory over Carlisle United. I bowed out in front of our own fans a couple of weeks later in a 1-0 FA Cup defeat at the hands of Derby County.

That season was also always going to be special as the club gave me the honour of having a testimonial year. Again, it was Mr Fix-It Howard Stephenson who came up with the idea that the club should show its appreciation for my decade of service and I was delighted when they said yes. My priorities were still on the field but there was also plenty to enjoy off it as Howard organised a series of functions including dinners, a day at the races, golf day and men-only events with strippers. The latter provided some interesting memories, not least Ray Lewington, Colin Morris and Paul Stancliffe dressing up as The Three Degrees – I bet not too many people have a photograph of England's assistant boss, Lewington, as a woman!

Joe Bolton did his Shakin' Stevens impression pretty well and young goalkeeper John Burridge his conjuring act very badly! It was all great fun and typical of the way the club, players and fans bought into my big year. Thanks to Howard, the venues were always full and my year was a great success in every way, except for on the pitch.

I also enjoyed good social times and banter with former Liverpool and England skipper Emlyn Hughes, then manager of Rotherham United. I went to the Rising Sun pub at the top of Ecclesall Road on a Sunday and would often see Emlyn in there. Doctors, solicitors and other professionals tended to gather there and I thoroughly enjoyed the atmosphere. I liked and admired Emlyn a great deal. His achievements as a player had been fantastic, notably under the iconic Bill Shankley at Anfield, but he was always warm and approachable. He happily talked with anyone who popped in and wanted to share a few thoughts about the game. It was a good social outlet for me at a time when my future was up in the air. There is a common bond among footballers and I generally enjoyed the company of bright, witty guys away from the call of duty. Emlyn asked me a number of times to play for him at Millmoor which was nice, although I still hadn't given up hope of staying at Bramall Lane. When it came to the crunch though, the fact Hughes and Porterfield, whom he'd taken over from at Rotherham, didn't see eye-to-eye meant it was a non starter.

The mid-season tour to Seville was also more memorable as a social occasion rather than the football. The fun started when a number of us, Stancliffe, McNaught and Withey included, were in the VIP lounge waiting to fly to Gibraltar and then onto Spain. Most people recognise that feeling of being a little nervous and bored waiting for a flight, so when Withey suggested we should get out of there and find a bar, I was among the takers. One pint quickly became four or five before we heard an urgent message over the tannoy for the last travellers to quickly board the plane.

Directors and other players had already bagged seats at the front, so the drinkers sat down towards the back. We decided the others were just being boring so continued with the session during the flight. Porterfield stood up and started to edge his way down the plane towards us. I thought we were in for a real bollicking for drinking too much and was preparing for the verbal onslaught. Much to my surprise he told me to nudge up and sat with us, saying he didn't want to be with that boring lot at the front!

The boss merrily joined in our drinking session before we landed in Gibraltar where his behaviour was even more amusing or bizarre, depending on where you were coming from. At the airport he opened his briefcase which we presumed was carrying important items for his trip. Imagine our faces when all it contained was a bottle of whisky. We then had to go barely 100 yards from the airport to our coach for the drive to Seville but Porterfield insisted on us joining him in a taxi. When we got there it would have been far better had we just been able to slip into our hotel unnoticed without any fuss. But unfortunately, the Mayor of Seville decided to greet us personally on arrival and came onto the coach. I'm not quite sure what he thought when Porterfield then landed him a smacker of a kiss on his lips!

On our return, I wasn't in the Blades side and Ian Porterfield suggested I go to Mansfield for a month. I still wanted to play for the first team and was looking forward to the climax of my testimonial season, a game with Wednesday at Bramall Lane, so I wasn't keen. Yet there was nothing much to lose from going there for a chat – after all, it wasn't a million miles from Sheffield.

*****

I was doing my best to be open minded when I pulled up at the small, fairly rundown Field Mill ground. Manager Ian Greaves, who had worked wonders at Bolton Wanderers, was in his office. Without any introduction, he asked whether I wanted a cup of tea. When I said yes, he took his teabag out of his cup and put it in mine. That told me a lot about the guy – here was a down-to-earth bloke I could get on with.

In walked club coach Billy Dearden, who I knew well from Sheffield United when he was scoring goals in the First Division at around the time I arrived. It was great to see a familiar face and I was in no doubt who marked the manager's card! I liked the next thing Greavesie told me too. He said: 'You know, there's something wrong at this club at the moment – we haven't had a fight in training for a fortnight!'

He said they were having a really good go at getting out of the Fourth Division and I hadn't been getting too many games at Sheffield United. So why didn't I sign on for a month, get some games under my belt, and start enjoying my football again? I'd be much appreciated at the football club, he told me, as he continued to sell the temporary move to me. He had a good point and I agreed straightaway.

Those were good times for Mansfield as they had some very useful players in their squad. My first day's training at Field Mill was an even bigger culture shock however. I went from being pampered at Bramall Lane to a virtual free-for-all. When we arrived for training in the morning, everything was laid out ready for us. Our kit was all neatly hung up with items such as towels and socks individually numbered. In addition, each player had a number which roughly reflected our seniority – the nearer you got to number one, the higher you were. I was number 47 when I arrived but got right up to number two by the time I moved to Mansfield. That was top dog as number one was reserved for the goalkeeper. In contrast at Mansfield, we'd be in the dressing room and one of the apprentices would come in with a bag full of kit and balls which he'd throw into the middle. There was then a frenzy as all the lads tried to find themselves matching kit. Needless to say, it often didn't work that way and I ended up with one green and one red sock. But I soon got to like it.

I'd not been at Field Mill long when news came through that Porterfield had got the sack. He lost his way after a fantastic start in the hot seat, and although we were not in any danger of being relegated from the Second Division, it didn't come as a total shock. The new manager was Billy McEwan, who'd earlier worked on the coaching side at Bramall Lane. I still very much regarded myself as a Sheffield United player, so much so that I drove back from Mansfield after training to have my dinner at Bramall Lane. I had no intention of leaving Sheffield United permanently if I could help it.

There were one or two early injury problems and Billy raised my hopes by saying he intended to recall me from my loan before the end of the season. But I heard no more and saw the campaign out with Mansfield Town, playing a small part in their promotion to the Third Division as Stags finished in third spot behind Chester City and champions Swindon Town.

My testimonial match was becoming an even more emotional occasion as I realised it was likely to be my very last 90 minutes in the famous red and white. It was good of Wednesday to bring a side although the friendliness would end once the first whistle blew! The people of Sheffield, mostly Blades fans, did me proud as more than 10,000 turned out, a very good attendance for what everyone else regarded as a 'friendly'.

Howard was on the job ensuring my big night went well – but, for once, his PR stunt went badly wrong. It was almost comical when I think back on it, although I wasn't nearly so thrilled at the time. Howard thought it would be good for my sponsored car, a black Mazda RX7 from Woodseats Motors, to be driven round the pitch. It got a good reception from Blades fans but a very different response from Owls fans behind the goal who pelted it so mercilessly with coins that it was more black and white when I saw it again. The driver said the noise was so bad he thought he'd gone deaf.

Lane legend Tony Currie and Simon Stainrod, with whom I shared some of my best early days with the Blades, returned to play, with my mate Emlyn Hughes also making a guest appearance alongside first team stars such as Keith Edwards, Colin Morris and Kevin Arnott. The Owls welcomed back Paul Hart, Gary Megson, Lee Chapman and Brian Marwood and popular Sheffield-based boxer Herol 'Bomber' Graham kicked the game off for us.

We won the match 4-3 with me scoring my final goal for the Blades with a header. Most people probably assumed it was the usual case of allowing the beneficiary to cap off his big night but I'm telling you it wasn't that way at all. I got decent contact on the ball and there was nothing Wednesday goalkeeper Martin Hodge could do about it. That was one great memory for me to take from my farewell.

The other highlight earned me a swift rebuke from Marwood. There he was going down the wing doing a fancy dan overstep and probably thinking he was safe from a TK special. Too wrong, mate. That was just the sighter I needed. This was my last ever chance to leave my stamp on an Owl and I took it perfectly. I launched into the striker with a scything tackle that took him over the advertising boards. 'What are you doing? It's only a friendly,' he snapped, as he eventually got back to his feet. 'Not to me!' I replied, soaking in the moment.

Some people moaned about it afterwards, calling me every name under the sun, but that was the way I played my football and I wasn't going to change, even in my own testimonial. I've had plenty of positive dealings with Brian since in his capacity with the Professional Footballers' Association, and I'm glad to say we still have a good laugh about that incident. There were no hard feelings between the two of us, that's for sure. I handed my Blades shirt to a grateful fan after the final whistle and very suddenly it really was all over. I genuinely felt very sad and mixed up on what was generally a successful and happy occasion.

It was the end of the season and with my month's loan at Mansfield Town at an end, my future was totally up in the air. This was the first time my contract had run into its final year but I still hoped against hope that Sheffield United would extend my deal after it ended in June. I knew Greavesie was keen to take me permanently and there was interest, too, from another former Blade colleague. Danny Bergara was first team coach to manager Bruce Rioch at Middlesbrough who were going through hard times. They were in the Third Division and at one stage had even been thrown out of Ayresome Park. Danny asked me to come over and have a chat with Rioch. The Boro boss wanted to sign me as a left back but warned there'd be no signing on fee or bonuses. The idea was to get the club promoted back out of the Third Division, then there'd be more money on the table. That side of things didn't bother me too much. The sticking point was the 108 mile door-to-door journey. I had a good house in Sheffield and didn't want to up sticks to Teeside, so I turned Boro down.

The next few weeks were the saddest of my whole career with Sheffield United and left a very bitter taste in my mouth. Of course, I knew the score. I was out of contract, having not played too many games in that final season as I continued to battle against injury. Also, I'd just been sent out on loan to another club. But the way in which the club finished me was really disappointing. All I got was a very brief letter through the post from acting chairman Derek Dooley saying thanks for my service to the club but my contract was not going to be renewed.

It was the bog standard letter a player who had been at the club for a year or been with us on loan might expect. But I'd been at the football club for ten years and just had a testimonial. I'd always given 100 per cent, remained loyal to the Blades through thick and thin, and put body and soul on the line for the cause. I didn't disagree with their verdict that it was time for me to move on, however much I wanted to stay. I just think inviting me in for a cup of coffee and thanking me in person would have been more appropriate. I'm not really blaming the club as a whole for the way I was treated. I'm sure Blades stalwarts John Short or John Harris would have ensured I was given a better send off had they been around

What happened next made things worse. I got a telephone call from my mate Howard Stephenson asking me to go down to the club to chat with Dooley. What could this be about? As I walked through the door I noticed commercial manager Andy Daykin, a guy I'd spent quite a bit of time with socially, was looking embarrassed. Perhaps it was the letter and the way they handled my departure that was on his mind. When I sat down in Dooley's office, he came quickly to the point. The club was due to go to Guernsey for an end of season tour, a trip I would now miss as I was no longer on their books. He explained that the Blades didn't have any ready cash to cover daily expenses and as I'd just had monies from my testimonial, could I kindly help the club out by lending them £5,000?

I was taken aback by the Blades' plight and the fact they were asking me for a favour so soon after ditching me. But I instantly agreed nevertheless. To be fair, the club kept their side of the bargain. They promised to repay me quickly on their return and they did. I received the £5,000 back partly through a cheque and the rest in cash. That issue was sorted with no harm done.

But when I needed a favour soon afterwards as Greavesie stepped up his bid to take me permanently to Mansfield it was a different story. He asked me to sign for them but said Stags couldn't afford a signing on fee. His idea was for Mansfield to pay £20,000 to the Blades, who could then make an ex-gracia payment to me to save Stags paying the tax.

So I went to Bramall Lane to ask Dooley if he could help. When I got to the ground that had been home for so many years, I was told the chairman was busy. No problem, I thought, I'll wait until he is able to see me. When I walked in, his desk was full of paperwork and he was fairly distracted. I put Greavesie's proposal to him and he said that wasn't something the club could help with. Again, it wasn't the answer I was annoyed about, but the bloke's manner. He didn't appear to be really listening and gave me no reason. Had he said he'd like to help and explained why he couldn't, I'd have left having felt I'd been attended to. Sadly, that wasn't the case. 'You've got a short memory,' I said, as I walked out of the Bramall Lane door for the very last time.

Leaving Sheffield United as a player was a huge moment in my life. If you read the *Sheffield Star* from time to time, you'd have got the idea that I had asked for a transfer from Bramall Lane in the past because I couldn't wait to sign for a First Division side. It was reported that I was frustrated that the Blades had slipped so far down the football ladder and I couldn't fulfil my true potential there. Understandable though those sentiments were, I can assure you they were all rubbish. I was upset by the way I was treated on occasions but, had I wanted to go elsewhere whilst in my prime, I had endless opportunities to do so. Offers from Leeds, Forest, Spurs, Derby County, Luton Town and Norwich City among others were real enough.

To be honest, I lost count of the amount of times clubs either came in for me or were linked with me in the press. Most of it just went over my head because Sheffield United was always my club. Even if agents had come on the scene earlier – I did have some contact with a guy called Gerry Webster after Ian Porterfield had taken over – it wouldn't have made any earthly difference. Nobody was ever going to tell me to sign for another football club.

Some people said the fact I stayed at Bramall Lane showed I wasn't ambitious enough. I'd say the opposite. I was actually over ambitious in that I believed I could achieve all my goals at Sheffield United. I was convinced for many years that we would regain the First Division status we lost under Jimmy Sirrel and, yes, I was gutted both for the club and for myself that it never happened whilst I was there. I blanked Neville Kaye's stark warnings and fought tooth and nail to get myself back on that pitch to try and make my personal dreams come true. But eventually you just have to accept there's nothing more you can do – my Sheffield United playing days really were all over.

Seaside special: first snap of a young TK with brother Terry on
holiday with Mum and Dad

Now for the full Kenworthy
clan: yours truly, Terry and
younger sister Julie …

Boot camp before going our separate ways – big brother Terry was due to emigrate to New Zealand whilst I was preparing for life with the Blades

TK (bottom left) with Blades Youth as a 15-year-old schoolboy

On tour with Jimmy Sirrel (second left, back row) at a youth tournament in Holland. Players include Simon Stainrod, Keith Edwards and Paul Garner whilst right at back is John Short, who signed me for Blades, alongside youth team coach Dave Turner

VIᵉ TOURNOI EUROPÉEN JUNIORS DE MONACO — 12 - 19 NOVEMBRE 1976
CHALLENGE PRINCE ALBERT

Alongside stars of the future with England Youth in Monte Carlo. Big names I played with included Gordon Cowans, Derek Statham, Sammy Lee, Chris Woods, Ricky Hill and our own Simon Stainrod

Norman Hunter mark II. The press posed this photo to build up the image before we faced each other in the First Division at Elland Road

Never knew it at the time but I broke my back in this Anglo Scottish tie with Dundee at Bramall Lane. Barry Butlin (also pictured) was one who shared my pain

Former England maverick Frank Worthington marks me at a flag kick for Birmingham City at Bramall Lane. Stewart Houston, the ex-Manchester United defender, is my fellow Blade

Next to a legend – Cec Coldwell, of course, a Blade through and through.
Oh, yes, on my other side is Martin Peters

Greyhounds were a passion – and still are. At Owlerton with
Paul Stancliffe and Tony Philliskirk and my great mate Howard
Stephenson on my right

Celebrating a crucial goal with defensive partner and mate John MacPhail

Going up, up, up. My towering header against Posh helps clinch promotion from the Fourth Division as my Bramall Lane rollercoaster begins to turn

Anything they can do – friend and rival Terry Curran, then a Blade, and Neil Whatmore, prolific scorer and later a mate at Mansfield, are in focus but it's me scoring for Blades against Oxford

Being a hard tackler often got me into trouble with referees. Here I'm receiving a booking in an Anglo Scottish tie

Tale of two clubs? I'm playing here against Mansfield but wasn't nearly so comfortable when roles were later reversed

England left back Kenny Sansom, then of Crystal Palace, tries to block a Kenworthy blast

Off field rivalry as I take part in a pancake challenge with a Sheffield Wednesday official. Fortunately, Radio Hallam DJ Dave Kilner (left) was a big Blades fan

Enjoying a happy hour chatting with pop legend and Watford chairman Sir Elton John after a concert in Sheffield

You beauty! Alex Sabella, now Argentina manager, and Mickey Speight cradle Miss Sheffield United. But I was never far behind with the ladies

With Keith Edwards
at a function – the
goalscorer supreme
helped me when I
needed it most

A double against
Tranmere was
the perfect
remedy after
missing a spot
kick against
Mansfield.
My secret was
to pick my
favourite corner
and stick to it

Smashing a goal past Wrexham and Wales goalkeeper Dai Davies at
Bramall Lane

We're going up – Blades celebrate Fourth Division promotion with
boss Ian Porterfield

Move over The Three Degrees – Ray Lewington, now England assistant manager, Colin Morris and Paul Stancliffe, get into the spirit for my testimonial. I'm in yellow and you can also spot John Burridge

Boxer Herol Bomber Graham tosses the coin at my testimonial as I look on with Owls goalkeeper Martin Hodge

Testimonial evening at Bramall Lane with, from left, owner Reg Brealey, Tony Currie, Derek Dooley, whom I was soon to clash with, and Paul Woolhouse, who did a Lord Lucan after taking over as chairman

Holding up the Freight Rover Trophy with the real hero of Wembley, goalkeeper Kevin Hitchcock, the best number one I played with

Spot of joy but, as Paul Garner and Tony Lowrey pile in, all I wanted to do was get back up!

Winning the Freight Rover Trophy with Stags was a surprise highlight in the twilight of my career

A very hard earned drink with Stags mate Keith Cassells after Wembley.
My eye tells some of the story but victory and having our own barman
eased the pain

Celebration time for family and friends – Mum Rita gets her hands on the
Freight Rover Trophy watched by my Dad Terry, long-term Blades official
and mate Andy Daykin (left) and Billy Dearden, Stags assistant manager
and Blades legend

Still on the football scene – I'm in the background behind the 'special one' Jose Mourinho working for Premier League Productions at a Newcastle versus Chelsea match at St James' Park

With Def Leppard's Joe Elliott, a true Blade, after a concert in Manchester in 2011. I never took that pen honest!

Enjoying a return to Bramall Lane with wife Jacqueline and children
Sofie and Wil in the 2012/13 season

Going back to the Lane is always a great time for the Kenworthy
family where Ted Hemsley, Tony Currie and Len Badger are
fellow Legends of the Lane

6

Wembley Dream and a Prison Nightmare

NO DISRESPECT to Mansfield Town but going to Field Mill was the furthest thing from my mind during my decade at Sheffield United. I turned down some of the biggest clubs in the land to stay with a set up that was in a different universe facilities-wise to the modest Nottinghamshire outfit. Having said all that, I had a fantastic time with Greavesie and co.

I enjoyed a totally unexpected career highlight, playing at Wembley and even scoring the winner! Someone up there was looking after me sending me the way of Greavesie, as he was right up my street. He'd taken Bolton Wanderers back into the First Division, after a series of near misses and handled top players such as Frank Worthington, Sam Allardyce and Peter Reid, before landing the supposed 'big job' at Wolverhampton Wanderers. Things didn't quite go to plan there, but it was still a surprise to see a manager of his pedigree in the lower divisions. Mansfield Town pulled off a coup when they hired Ian Greaves, that's for sure.

No airs, no graces, Greavesie was a true down-to-earth manager and, without doubt, the best I ever played for, with no disrespect to the bosses I rated highly at Bramall Lane. He courted a great atmosphere between the lads, approached the game with passion and treated players like adults. He was held in total respect by everyone in the dressing room. He was a big guy who knew how to handle himself.

Forever puffing his pipe, Greavesie was a genuinely good coach who was there every day on the training ground whilst leaving the drills and tactical side of how to overcome our next opponents to Billy Dearden. This was no Haslam and Bergara arrangement but two people pulling together much more equally to get the job done. Greavesie, the master manager whose record spoke for itself and Billy, Mr Mansfield Town, a terrific guy who knew the game inside out and was liked by everyone at the club. They fostered a camaraderie in that dressing room that spoke volumes. I'd known players within a team go their separate ways, but here they were all fighting for the same cause.

His other 'secret' at Field Mill was he had some very good players. I'll start with Kevin Hitchcock between the sticks because he was also the best I ever lined up in front of. Never given a first team opportunity at Cloughie's Forest, Kevin was a street fighter who found his feet at Field Mill. I thought so much of the guy I told Porterfield to go out and buy him and it was no surprise to me he ended up at Chelsea when Porterfield became manager. He was a snip at £190,000, believe me, because he could have played First Division or Premier Division football any day of the week.

The rock in the Stags defence was George Foster, another big man who served the club well for many years. I found out just how good he was at Field Mill by playing alongside him in defence but, unfortunately, we never hit it off as people. As in any successful team, we had players who could score goals. Neil Whatmore was a prolific striker under Greavesie at Burnden Park and still knew where the goalposts were, while Keith Cassells, who became one of my best friends at Mansfield, was a speed merchant who terrified the life out of defenders.

Our joy came during my first full season with the Stags as we consolidated our new status in the Third Division with a mid-table finish. It was in that most unfashionable of competitions – the cup for third and fourth divisions clubs then called the Freight Rover Trophy.

It was an adventure that crept up on us. Our focus was on how well we were going to fare in the league when we kicked off in the group stage (yes, I know it sounds like the Champions League!). Had we known what lay ahead in the following months, we would never have signed deals offering us £250 per player to get to Wembley and land the trophy. During those preliminary stages and the first couple of rounds, the Twin Towers never crossed our minds.

I come from the old school who treat every game as very important but there was little hint of the excitement to come when we went 2-0 down to Halifax Town after just eight minutes of our opening game at Field Mill. Dave Longhurst helped himself to a couple of goals and then missed a series of chances to complete his hat trick – had he done so, our Wembley dream would almost certainly have been over there and then. Things didn't seem any more promising when Keith Cassells missed a first half penalty and saw another effort cleared off the line. Cup runs, however, throw up all kinds of heroes and Jeff Chandler, on loan from Derby County, proved just such a man.

He returned to the Baseball Ground shortly after our two group games but did more than enough in his short time with us to see us through to the first round. He pulled a goal back just before half time and Neil Whatmore, troubled throughout that season with injury, set up Kevin Kent for a 65th minute equaliser that ensured we went to Millmoor to face Rotherham United in good heart. Again, we made things hard for ourselves in South Yorkshire when Kevin Hitchcock made an early mistake to allow Gareth Evans to give the Millers the lead and Whatmore missed a sitter.

But, with us needing at least a draw to make progress, it was Chandler who came up with a moment of magic in the 33rd minute when he cleverly bent a shot around teenage goalkeeper Giles Newcombe from the left hand side to bring us back onto level terms. Newcombe's heroics apart, we could have eased our nerves by winning the tie, but 1-1 proved just enough to see us through.

We then faced a series of away matches on the road to Wembley, although that wasn't too much of a disadvantage as we generally played better away from Field Mill that season. It was a very tough battle at York where Greavesie recalled vintage duo Neil Whatmore and former Blade Paul Garner and saw his selection pay off big time. Whatmore nudged us ahead with a typical goal in the 15th minute and both Keith Cassells and Mark Kearney had chances to put us out of sight. Yet we were indebted that night to the outstanding goalkeeping of Kevin Hitchcock as he kept the York strikers at bay. We had our hearts in our mouths in the very last minute when Keith Walwyn had an effort blocked on our goal line but held on for a gritty 1-0 victory.

The Area Quarter Final at Gigg Lane against Bury was another example of Greavesie's ability to adapt to different circumstances. We had problems dealing with Shakers striker Liam Robinson, who scored twice in their surprise 3-1 league victory at Field Mill a few weeks earlier, so the boss opted for a three-man central defence with Gary Pollard coming into the side to play alongside George Foster and myself. The result was that Bury rarely got through to Kevin Hitchcock as we took a firm grip on the tie. Our two goals were a contrast but equally as valuable. Kevin Kent scrambled us in front just before half time before Tony Lowery, who had a great game in midfield, thumped in a 25-yard volley to make it 2-0 shortly afterwards. Bury got a goal back 10 minutes from the end through Nigel Greenwood and once again it was all hands to the defensive pump in a tense finale as they went for an equaliser. Fortunately, we had an extra pair with our formation and held on to squeeze through 2-1.

The Boro match in the Northern Area semi final was probably when we realised we could have a worthwhile cup run on our hands. That wasn't arrogance on our part, I might add, but because of the clear message bombarding us from Bruce Rioch's side. As we settled at a cold and dark Ayresome Park, banners claiming 'Boro are on the way to Wembley' were all around us. The tie was always going to be a major challenge against Rioch's promotion chasing side who, probably rightly, considered themselves to be the biggest team in the competition. They were in third place and had only lost three times on their own patch,

I was particularly keen to put in a good display that night as I'd nearly signed for Rioch at the start of the season. But, instead of playing for my former Blades team mate, I lined up alongside George Foster at the heart of the Stags defence after Greavesie told the press what a brilliant record he had at Boro as both a player and a manager. He proved the master of mind games with that one.

The atmosphere among the home crowd was particularly hostile. I remember watching Kevin Hitchcock trotting towards his goal for the beginning of the match as coins rained against his goal frame. Not that we were ever going to be frightened. Looking around our dressing room and seeing good experienced players in our line up, I knew we would keep our heads. Greavesie may not have shouted our talents from the rooftops during that cup run yet he sat on the touchline knowing we had enough on that pitch to have a reasonable chance wherever we went. We fancied ourselves to give Liverpool a game, let alone Boro.

The home side had plenty of possession but our 1-0 win was thoroughly deserved as we limited Kevin Hitchcock's saves to a minimum. Instead, the best first half chances fell to Neville Chamberlain who scraped the bar with one good effort and forced Boro goalkeeper Stephen Pears into a good stop with another. The same pattern continued in the second half before we got the all-important breakthrough in the 73rd minute. Keith Cassells was scythed down in the penalty box by Tony Mowbray, now the Boro manager. Only the bravest could bear to look as up strode Mark Kearney to fire the spot kick home.

Understandably, Boro upped the pressure as time ran out and we had our hearts in our mouths about 30 seconds before the final whistle when Gary Gill had the ball in our net. The pressure was on as home supporters bayed for blood and it was a brave decision by the linesman to raise his flag for offside. Hundreds of Stags fans who had made the long journey, celebrated in style. I had a really good game, being given the man of the match award, which was particularly satisfying. Rioch was very sporting afterwards as he praised us for our performance and, yes, excitement was now beginning to mount in the town about the competition.

That put Mansfield through to the Northern Area Final for the second time in three seasons, with locals wondering if we could go one better and make it all the way to Wembley. Chester arrived at Field Mill for the first leg after winning 3-2 at our place in a league game a few days earlier and I was out injured. Almost 8,000 fans turned out, showing how the competition was now grabbing the imagination of the public. It was our first and only home tie in that famous cup run after the first game against Halifax and we quickly ensured they weren't going to go home disappointed. Yet again our astute manager came up with the goods with his selection. Ian Stringfellow had been out of the side but Greavesie decided to recall him after scoring a hat trick in the reserves. The striker gave us the all-important opening goal of the tie and it looked like our confident, attacking football was going to blow the visitors aside when Keith Cassells pounced on an error to make it 2-0 at the start of the second half. But in the last half hour Chester did enough to show the second leg would be no formality. We were grateful to full back Mike Graham for blocking two goalbound efforts to protect our two-goal advantage.

The press reported I was angry not to be included in the starting line up for the second leg at Sealand Road but they were wide of the mark. Greavesie was too good a manager to leave me out without finding out my feelings. It had taken me a fair amount of time to get fit again following an injury and I was just about ready. The boss took me aside in the hotel to ask whether I was 100 per cent. Had I said 'yes', I'm pretty sure he'd have pencilled me into the side but I was totally honest when I told him I wasn't quite ready to play a full 90 minutes. Greavesie named me as substitute, but could never have guessed I'd be on the pitch after just eight minutes – and in very unfortunate circumstances. Our left back Paul Garner was taken off the field after a shattering collision with Milton Graham which resulted in a free kick being awarded to Chester. My former Blades team mate, however, got much the worst of it and was led off with a fractured cheekbone, with me filling in at left back. My first task was to stand in the wall and see Colin Woodthorpe hammer in a 20-yarder to give Chester a 1-0 lead on the night and reduce our overall advantage to 2-1. We knew from that most traumatic of starts we were up against it and would need every ounce of effort and concentration to see the job through.

Our 3,500 travelling fans endured some scary first half moments as Chester poured forward in search of the equaliser. Their leading scorer, Gary Bennett, missed one good chance before seeing Tony Lowery block another effort and Kevin Hitchcock keep out the rebound. Then came my special moment on the stroke of half time. Another Chester effort looked to be sailing into our net but I stretched everything to get my head to it in the nick of time and clear it off the line.

The message in our dressing room at half time was loud and clear. We had to win it, not only for the fans but for Paul Garner, who was being driven home by taxi to Sheffield. The second half was a tense affair although there weren't that many direct threats on our goal. There were a couple of late flurries from the home side – as always during that knife-edge of a cup run – but, when the final whistle blew, reality started to set in. Mansfield Town were at Wembley for the first time in the club's long history. I was going to the Twin Towers for the first time in my playing career and was delighted to be fit and well to take my place in the cup final.

Excitement in the town grew greater and greater as we approached the big day against the holders, Terry Cooper's Bristol City, in front of more than 58,000 fans – a record for the competition – on Sunday, May 24 1987. Fans turned out in their thousands to support us and we were desperate to make their day. The Bristol players were on £15,000 each compared with our £250, a sign perhaps of how greatly they valued the competition after tasting glory 12 months previously.

To everyone's delight, Garner won his fitness battle to win back his place and I was selected in my favourite centre back position alongside George Foster with right back Mickey Graham completing our back four. We were in the 'home' or England dressing room. Could that be a lucky omen on this day of all days for Mansfield Town Football Club?

There were a couple of particularly familiar faces in the City side – big Keith Waugh, who always reminded me of a copper for some reason, between the sticks and my old sparring partner John MacPhail at the heart of the defence. Considering himself a Wembley veteran no doubt, Waugh told me to 'enjoy it' before the match which is always good advice. Such occasions often flash by so quickly and you're too caught up in the stress and tension to take it in. MacPhail was in a good mood, too. Good job I was far enough away not to get caught by one of his 'specials'

My final was nearly over before it had properly begun as I was injured by striker Glyn Riley's elbow inside the first five minutes. It split my eye wide open with Hitchcock screaming to get me attention. Billy Dearden took one look and told me to come off. I said he must be joking because I hadn't kicked the ball yet so I had six stitches put in and battled on. Foster and I fought hard against their strikers that afternoon. He took the brunt of the physical menace of former Scotland international Joe Jordan and did a fantastic job. We went off at half time with the final scoreless and balanced on a knife edge and never heard a word of Greavesie's interval talk. I was busy having eight more stitches to ensure the eye didn't open up again. The treatment finished just in time for me to go back up the tunnel and start again.

Kevin Kent drew first blood by shooting us ahead in the 56th minute from a cross by Keith Cassells, and Ian Stringfellow was within an ace of making it 2-0 midway through the second half when his header hit the bar. But City were always a threat themselves with David Moyes, now Manchester United's new manager, and Riley forcing the best out of Hitchcock before finally getting the better of our defence to level with just three minutes left.

Jordan, who had played at Wembley six times previously without being on the winning side, went close to winning it for City in the last minute. Despite that miss we were gutted. To be that close to winning any match, let alone a Wembley final, was tough to take but we had to raise ourselves again for 30 minutes of extra time with the prospect of a first-ever Wembley penalty shootout. Cassells was still causing them problems with his pace and Stringfellow saw the best chance saved by my former Blades colleague Keith Waugh, but there was no dividing two tiring sides.

It had been a very good and even cup final, but someone had to win and someone had to lose. Greavesie came across to sort out who was going to take the penalties and asked whether I wanted to be one of the five. I'd have jumped at the chance but was really struggling physically through a mixture of injury and exhaustion and held my hand up to tell him so. 'Leave me out, boss,' I said. 'But if it goes to sudden death, put me down for the first one.' Greavesie nodded. The downside of penalty shootouts is that there are always victims.

Cassells had an excellent game but when he had his penalty saved by Waugh in the shootout, it was odds on City to win it. That was when Hitchcock came to the party. He had to save Gordon Owen's kick to keep us in the contest, although there was bound to be pressure on the City player as he'd missed a spot kick only a couple of weeks previously in the play offs. Amid almost unbearable tension, Hitchcock managed somehow to divert Owen's effort over the bar to keep us in with a chance. Then Kevin Kent stepped up with the world on his shoulders and put his spot kick away to level the scores at 4-4.

I was sat on the touchline barely able to take in what was happening with my socks rolled down and my injured calves virtually screaming but Neil Whatmore, substituted during the final, was watching very closely and thought he'd spotted something useful. He told me my former colleague Waugh had dived left each time and I should call his bluff and chip him. Just imagine that. The most important moment in Mansfield Town's history and I should knock in the cheekiest of spot kicks!

First to shoot in sudden death was David Moyes attempting to put City back into the lead. But again Hitchcock proved our hero by pulling off another fine save. Greavesie was as good as his word and it was now down to me. I can hardly tell you how I felt approaching that ball. My calves were on fire as I walked towards a goal getting smaller and smaller with every step. I was a combination of pain and nerves and did my best to get eye contact with Waugh. I wanted to know he was feeling as desperate as I was. But he kept his eyes away from me and spread his arms as wide as possible. It looked like his goal had disappeared. I certainly couldn't see any of it. I took a couple of deep breaths and collected my thoughts. Whatmore's words went through my mind but there was no way I was going to risk a chip. Waugh had dived to his left and knew from our days at Bramall Lane that was where I liked to put my penalties. I knew what a good record he had of saving spot kicks and couldn't risk him diving early that way and saving it. I told myself just to concentrate on getting a decent connection and aim slightly to his right. My mind was made up, changing it could be fatal. I ran up and saw Waugh begin to move to his left as I struck the ball. I knew in that split second I was going to score. My shot was low and true, just right of centre. The ball was in the back of the net. We'd done it! We'd won the Freight Rover Trophy.

I sunk to my knees – not in prayer, but because my legs couldn't hold me a moment longer. All hell was let loose. Mansfield players rushed in my direction to celebrate. First Tony Lowery, then Keith Cassells. Lads were climbing on top of me when all I wanted to do was stand up! I was in real pain but couldn't blame them. Somehow I was helped to my feet and hobbled off the pitch into the sanctuary of the dressing room. George Foster said afterwards the atmosphere in there was 'deadly quiet' and he was right. Many of us were physically spent and soaking up the enormity of the moment. I glanced around that dressing room and saw familiar faces – Keith Cassells, Neil Whatmore, Paul Garner and Foster himself. Over the years I had both played with and against these players, each of whom didn't have many football miles left in their tanks. We'd all been on long journeys and now it had come to this. I looked at Greavesie and Billy Dearden and thought what this meant to them. I felt particularly happy for Greavesie, on the eve of his 55th birthday,who deserved to go into the record books as a Stags legend after guiding the club to a first trophy in an 82-year history. Apart from giving everyone at the club a day they will never forget for the rest of their lives, Mansfield scooped about £100,000 from winning that competition, serious cash for the club and enough to ease the annual financial struggle. It was a huge, huge moment in my football career and in my life. Thank goodness I hadn't listened to Neville Kaye. His advice may have been good, but it was worth all the pain and disappointment to be in that winning Wembley dressing room.

*****

If the shining highlight of my Mansfield Town career came on the pitch, there was a terrible shock off it just a few months later. Among the many folk who had congratulated me was my great mate Howard. The reason I recall the incident so clearly was that, through nobody's fault, we'd begun to drift apart in recent months. I was now at Field Mill rather than Bramall Lane and Howard had gone in an unexpected direction too. He'd become a director at Stockport County, a strange move until you realise the invitation had come from chairman Brendon Ellwood, also a huge Blades fan.

Niggles were beginning to form in my mind about my testimonial. Dealing with the financial side is no quick task and I wasn't concerned in any way when I received an intial payment into my bank account. But as weeks and months ticked by and there was still money outstanding, I got a call that started my head spinning. I was told out of the blue that Howard was deep in financial trouble and that I should check with him what was happening. It didn't seem possible. Howard always had fast cash in his pocket, there'd never been any question he was a man of financial means. Suddenly it began to click – the money had dried up, but his lifestyle hadn't. Howard had been borrowing from Peter to pay Paul and spiralling into trouble. I spoke with him briefly about my testimonial cash and he gave me a typical, instant Howard-style answer that everything was fine and being sorted out. Then came the hammer blow that broke my heart.

I received a phone call telling me Howard had committed suicide. I met up with Gail as soon as I could and discovered some of the grim truth. He had gone to a hotel in Sheffield, hired a car and driven into Derbyshire, where he attached a hosepipe to the exhaust of his car. He'd drunk half a bottle of whisky. Everything pointed to the fact that he'd made his decision. He'd made provision for all his policies to be paid out to Gail, including one insurance policy that would still be applicable even if he committed suicide. In addition, he'd written a series of letters, presumably explaining what was in his tortured mind. One was addressed to me. Gail handed me the letter and, in a moment of complete madness, I tore it into little pieces. Perhaps I was angry at the way he had gone, I don't know. But tearing up that letter without opening and reading it remains the biggest regret of my whole life. Bar none. I still think about it 25 years or more later. Why didn't I take the time to read what Howard had to say? I'll take that guilt and shame to the grave.

Money didn't matter. How could it? Had Howard told me his problem, I'd have gladly given it to him. But that's another reason why I feel so awful. When we were seeing each other regularly, he could never have kept such an important secret from me. He would have told me and we would have sorted it together. What went through the guy's mind in those weeks and months? It must have been dreadful beyond belief for him to decide it was better not to live. I'm talking about a person who, after Terry moved to

New Zealand, filled the role of an older brother. He was a diamond of a bloke, as big as a lion, but never hurt anyone. He left a huge hole in my life. I missed him the moment I heard of his death and I miss him just the same way now. Rest in peace, Howard, I'm so sorry ...

I may have been making a new start club-wise but couldn't beat my injury jinx. Another serious one came the following season in a Tuesday night match against Notts County at Field Mill. I was running back to nick the ball away from one of their forwards who brought his elbow back as he was trying to take a shot and caught me flush on the right side of my face. Next thing I remember was waking up in the dressing room and instinctively trying to sit up. I could make out that my shirt was covered in blood and my face was a mess. Alongside me was striker Keith Cassells, who had been in the treatment room. I could guess it was really bad as he was warning me not to touch my face but to wait for the ambulance.

I was taken to the cottage hospital in Mansfield where it became clear they didn't know what to do with me. After a lot of thought, it was agreed I should stay the night before being moved to the Northern General Hospital in Sheffield next day where Billy Dearden arranged for a professor to see me. Both my eyes were closed and they couldn't operate until the swelling went down. So they booked me in, gave me an x-ray and waited for a couple of days for things to improve. The extent of my accidental injury was becoming clear. My jaw was broken, eyesocket shattered, cheekbone fractured and the right side of my nose broken. Little wonder the nurse looking after me at the hospital thought I'd been in a car accident rather than playing football.

My cheekbone was like eggshell inside, my jaw had to be wired and my nose reassembled. Then to cap it all, I needed plastic surgery on my eye. After the operation, I woke up in a dark room with my face packed with gauze. I tried to pull it off me and it was full of clotted blood. The nurse came into the room and asked what I was doing – the gauze was stopping my nose from collapsing again.

I was in a real state for a fair time afterwards as my face was black and blue. When I attended football matches during my recovery, I looked a shocking sight, as the boys were only too quick to remind me. Some thought I'd never play again, but I got myself back on the field as Mansfield continued to battle away in the third flight. In 1987/88 we were grateful for a couple of good results towards the end to ensure our survival in 19th place in a division won by mighty Sunderland and also including the likes of Brighton and Fulham. I also played a good many games the following season – my final bow in league football – in which we finished a creditable 15th.

Out of the 46 league games that season, two stood out as soon as the fixtures were published – home and away against Sheffield United! I never thought I'd play against the Blades but relegation the previous season meant new manager Dave Bassett was competing with Mansfield in the third flight. When I say those fixtures stood out, I don't mean I was looking forward to them. No way. It was very difficult to play against the club I still considered my own. If I could have ducked out of playing in those matches, I would have done so. Imagine the shock to my system therefore when the draw was made for the first round of the FA Cup and we drew the Blades at Field Mill in November. It was a weird, weird feeling lining up to mark Brian Deane that cold Saturday and it didn't get any easier when the 90 minutes ended 1-1.

If there was anything harder on my emotions than that experience, it was the prospect of going back to Bramall Lane on the Tuesday night. I used to share transport with John Ryan, the former Wednesday full back, who lived in Manchester and pick up Steve Charles, who also lived in

Sheffield, on my way to Stags matches. But as I was still living in Sheffield, I drove into Bramall Lane on my own. I got into the main park – the place where I parked my car thousands of times on match days or for training and still considered to be home. 'Tony Kenworthy, Mansfield Town,' I said, the words still sounding a little strange as I approached the steward. 'There's no parking space for you,' he replied. 'Well, go and get me one,' I replied, feeling my anger rise. A phone call was made to Derek Dooley and the message was relaid to me. There was no parking space available, even though the ground was never going to be anywhere near full. I wasn't taking no for an answer. I just drove past the steward and parked my car in a reserved spot. I didn't care. I would have loved Dooley to come to the door and confront me so I could give it him both barrels. He asked me for a favour and I handed the club £5,000 of my money; I asked him twice for a good turn in return, including this very small one, and the answer was no. Don't talk to me about Dooley's statue outside Bramall Lane; I can only speak as I see it: Derek Dooley was a Wednesday man, he wasn't a Blade. He treated a guy who gave Sheffield United Football Club years of loyal service like rubbish. I was not impressed.

On the positive side, I had a good chat before the game with my former defensive partner Paul Stancliffe who was the Blades skipper. I bumped into very familiar faces among the office staff, including my good friend John Garrett. That didn't make playing the game any easier. Not at all. But professionalism took over and I did my best for Mansfield Town, the club paying my wages. I must have played reasonably well, too, because we pulled off a minor FA Cup shock by winning 2-1.

It was a very good night for the travelling Stags fans but I couldn't bring myself to share their delight. I felt numb about the whole experience. I'd just helped to knock my own club out of the world's most famous football competition. How crazy is that?

I enjoyed my time with the Stags, a great down-to-earth 'real' football club, but the writing was probably on the wall for me the day Greaves resigned in February 1989. We were on our way to staying in the Third Division for another season, no mean feat in itself, but he'd had enough. He'd served his time in management, he reckoned, and it was time to give someone else a go – unfortunately for me that man was George Foster.

Don't get me wrong, I respected George as a defender and as a Mansfield legend. I played alongside him in the centre of defence enough times to know what a rock he was and what a major influence he was in our dressing room. I had no problem with George as a player, none at all. But did I trust him as a person? No, I didn't. The reason was obvious – at least to me. For months and months, George had been worming his way into the good books and thoughts of club officials. Club rules were the same at Mansfield Town as they were elsewhere – players sat at the back of the coach and management at the front. Only problem was there was always one empty seat at the back – George's. He'd be at the front as if he was one of the bosses. That irritated me no end and I didn't hold back from telling him about it. In fact I reminded him to his face every time it happened. He just laughed. Here was the problem of promoting someone from within the dressing room. How was he going to react to a bloke who had taken the piss out of him at every opportunity? I didn't need an answer.

I had a lot of problems with my Achilles during that season and was in the treatment room when George asked pointedly how I was. I found it odd because he never usually asked about my welfare. When I said I was fine, he just went on his merry way. It was only two or three days later that George was appointed player-manager. He'd clearly known exactly what was going to happen when he had spoken to me. One of his first actions was to call me into his office for a chat. He asked whose side I was on. I wasn't sure exactly what he was getting at and he went on: 'Are you on my side?' I told him I was on my own side – I wasn't playing games with him. I didn't get on with him as a person. We may have been within a few yards of each other on a Saturday afternoon, but you'd never find the two of us sharing a drink at a bar.

I did play several games under George Foster towards the end of that season. Ironically, the two Blades games were within three short weeks of each other in April. Bassett's men were still looking for points to clinch promotion back to the Second Division at the first attempt and here was I standing in their way. I played in the first game at Field Mill which Blades won 1-0 but was genuinely out injured for the return clash at Bramall Lane. I sat in the stands that night watching 'my team' and the one I was contracted to. To be brutally honest, I was pleased enough when Blades got revenge for that FA Cup defeat with a 2-1 victory. Defeat wasn't going to hit Mansfield too hard in any case. I was just glad it was all over.

I was in a vulnerable position coming towards the end of my three-year contract with injury concerns still hanging over me. The fatal blow came when, still feeling my Achilles, I was advised to go out onto the training pitch and give it a try. The result was it went twang as if I'd been shot and I ended up in the Nuffield Hospital between Nottingham and Mansfield later that day having yet another operation. Needless to say there was no rehab on offer and I was still unfit and feeling particularly vulnerable when the inevitable chop arrived. Foster didn't have the spine to tell me I was no longer wanted face to face, so I was laid off with another 'Dear Tony' letter. This was the beginning of a very difficult time for me as the thought of what the hell was I going to do after my playing days first started to hit home. I was still under 30 years old, yet knew I was very close to the end of my football road

I took to the bottle to a certain extent to try to blot the feelings out and things could easily have gone further downhill before a former team mate did me a favour. Ex-Blade Peter Withe, then a coach at Huddersfield Town, asked whether I'd like to join up with them. The Terriers were managed by Eoin Hand and had a decent side including another Blades warhorse in Keith Edwards up front alongside emerging Welshman Iwan Roberts and Simon Charlton, formerly of Bolton, in midfield. Eventually I was offered a six-month contract which I was grateful for and gave me time to sharpen up. I had played a couple of reserve games and things were beginning to look up when I went into the club for training and was hit by a bolt from the blue.

The incident in question had happened over a year before whilst I was still with the Stags. I got a telephone call from a friend I met at the dogs called Mark Wastany, who ran his own DIY shop in Ecclesall Road in Sheffield and had built a conservatory at my house. He asked me to go out with him to watch a night's dog racing at Owlerton. It was a nice summer's evening in early June and we had a good night. I had a couple of drinks, but nothing too excessive, and was driving us back home to Sheffield in my brand new Nissan Skyline. We were approaching the traffic lights in Penistone Road when the madness began. Mark said we could just catch last orders if we were quick, which seemed a good idea to me. As I came up to the lights, they turned from green to amber and Mark shouted to 'go through them', which I instinctively did.

Just at that moment, I saw a Ford Escort on my right hand side and knew I was in trouble. The other car clipped the back of mine and spun it into the railings. His vehicle got the best of it, suffering just minor damage to the bumper whereas mine was in a mess. I had no complaints as the accident was clearly my fault. The lights changed when I was about 10 yards away and would probably have been on red by the time I drove through them. The other driver was driving totally legally and didn't do anything wrong.

To its credit, my Nissan, a very powerful car, somehow emerged from the crash well enough for me to drive it. It stalled and restarted and Mark urged me to try to get it to his shop. Stupidly, I agreed. We abandoned the wreckage before going into the back of the shop and phoning the police. Then I made my next catastrophic mistake. Out of sheer panic, I told them I'd been to the dogs and my vehicle had been stolen. It was absolutely crazy. They asked me to come down to the police station near Hillsborough where I was immediately put in a cell and confronted by three aggressive police officers with Mark being questioned in a separate room. It was obvious they'd had a report of an accident involving a car with a driver matching my description and thought I was to blame.

They stripped me to check for incriminating evidence but, luckily, there wasn't a mark on me. That could have changed, however, as the officers said that, unless I coughed up the truth, they'd give me a 'good leathering'. The choice wasn't very good, whether I confessed or not, I was still in for a good hiding. One officer was just a couple of inches from my face and the whole experience was very intimidating. They knew exactly who I was and being a fairly well known footballer wasn't in my favour. They thought I was a big shot lying through his teeth and determined to put me through it.

The whole thing was completely foreign to me. I'd never had any experience of dealing with the police apart from a couple of parking tickets and being manhandled in that way was a shock to my system. I really didn't know they treated people that way. Eventually, I asked for a solicitor and they had no alternative but to grant my request. When my legal man from Irwin Mitchell solicitors arrived, he told me to say nothing at all and, within half an hour or so, we were out of the station. I hadn't been charged with anything and was told I could go home. That was the end of the matter, I presumed, unless I heard anything different.

I did my best to put things right with the other driver, the innocent party in all this. The police told my solicitor the identity of the driver and I paid for repairs to his car which wasn't very much. The accident had also been reported in the local press. I'd done wrong but thought I'd paid for it. My new and very expensive vehicle was a complete write-off and the insurance company refused to pay out. So I lost the lot.

I didn't tell anyone else what had happened. Nobody had been injured and I paid the price for my foolishness – or so I thought. So I didn't say anything to my parents, Mansfield Town or Huddersfield when I later joined up with them. It was a good 15 months later in September 1989 when the bolt came out of the blue. The accident was right at the back of my mind and I was completely shocked when the Huddersfield secretary said my solicitor wanted me to call very urgently. I couldn't believe my ears when he said: 'You should have been in court last week. I have been trying to get hold of you.'

I hadn't been avoiding him. I just hadn't been at home in Sheffield very much as I was training full time at Huddersfield. He told me not to worry but a new court date had been fixed and I needed to come and see him. We arranged to meet next day. It wasn't the same solicitor but a big portly gentleman who put my mind partly at ease by insisting I had a good case. I was being charged with perverting the course of justice and not stopping after an accident, but somehow a very good witness had come forward whose story backed up my account. He was a Percy

Sugden-type character, a good egg who knew everything going on in his neck of the woods, and was convinced he'd seen my car park up outside his property at about 12.30am. The police had it on record I'd been locked up in their cells by 11pm, so this seemed a very lucky break for me as I was still sticking to my original story that my car had been stolen and I couldn't have been driving.

I had to take a couple of days off training with Huddersfield to attend my trial on a Wednesday and Thursday so was forced to tell the manager what was happening. I said I was due in court but it wasn't anything serious and I'd be back with the club on the Friday, which was what I honestly thought would happen. I made a similar phone call to my parents and, without going into too much detail, told them not to worry. Nevertheless, I was quite nervous when I turned up at Sheffield Crown Court for the start of the trial.

I saw the barrister working on my case and we chatted before the start. He told me that I'd get a fine if I pleaded guilty; but, if I continued to insist I was innocent, I could get a prison sentence even though this was unlikely. I've got to admit even the mention of jail frightened the life out of me however hard he tried to reassure me. Mark and I would have to make our own decision which way to go. But he insisted we had a very good witness who could swing the verdict in our favour. So we had a quick talk and decided we'd go for it and plead not guilty.

The opening of the case was strange. They brought seven men in to swear them into the jury – but all of them recognised me and had to be dismissed. Eventually a group of 12 was assembled, seven women and five men. I looked at all of them, my mind doing overtime. A strange thought hit me – if all 12 were Sheffield Wednesday fans, I'd not stand a prayer! Stupid thought, I know, but I wasn't thinking rationally as I was well out of my comfort zone. It was difficult to take much of what we saw on day one seriously.

The judge brought in a series of people to say their pieces and it seemed like a circus to the untrained eye.

Pick of the bunch, without doubt, was my witness who lived up to his billing as a stickler of a man. I was well pleased to have someone like him on my side. He told it as my barrister had said, being totally adamant my car pulled up at 12.30am. One problem with my story was there was no physical evidence of any break-in to my car and it wasn't the kind of vehicle you could just get into. On the other hand, the prosecution had no witnesses to say they'd seen the accident or me behind the wheel. I felt obliged to stick with my version of events, even though I knew it wasn't the truth. I didn't tell my legal team what really happened – not that they asked.

Wednesday's proceedings came to a close and it was time to go home. My eyes, however, had been drawn to a nice looking member of the CPS team – a legal secretary aged about 24 or 25. I approached her as we were walking out of court and asked how she felt it had gone. She said she wasn't allowed to discuss the case with me but did volunteer her opinion my witness had been particularly good. That cheered me up sufficiently to take the next step and ask if she'd like to go out for a drink after the case was done and dusted. She smiled and said 'yes', so I left the court that night feeling pretty pleased with myself.

I took even less notice of the evidence on day two. Nothing going on in front of me looked too serious. I convinced myself that, seeing as nobody had died and I hadn't taken any money, I was on reasonably safe ground. My barrister said the police and CPS had been gunning for me because I was a footballer and therefore had a high profile. When the evidence came to a sudden end and it took the jury just 40 minutes to reach their conclusion, we took that as a good sign. How wrong we were. As soon as I took my place back in the court room, I knew I was in trouble. I'd had quite a lot of eye contact with one of the female members of the jury during the case; now, as I fixed my gaze nervously on her, she made sure she didn't return my glance. My heart sank.

The first verdict was mine. When the foreman said 'guilty' I was in shock. I don't even recall him returning a similar verdict for Mark. Even then I didn't give a prison sentence a thought. Then the judge read out his sentence and it totally stunned me: nine months for perverting the course of justice and a further three for failing to stop. A total of 12 or was it nine? I hadn't taken on board whether the sentences were going to run consecutively or concurrently. All that mattered was the word 'prison' – I couldn't get it out of my mind. The guilty verdict totally changed my world and sent me into a mental whirl.

*****

You hear people talk a lot today about prison life being a doddle. But they're probably thinking more of folk so ingrained in the criminal system they are more 'at home' behind bars than in normal society. For me, it was a huge, huge blow to my system, not because of any damage to my ego but the sheer culture shock I went through at Armley.

Mark was led to a different cell and banged up along with people already convicted from other courts but the officer kept mine open. He immediately tried to help by suggesting people such as me shouldn't be sent to prison and marked my card about how bad and dangerous people were inside. I remember him saying it was certainly no hotel and would be full of low-lifes. I should keep my head down and my nose clean and he'd find me a job.

My identity as a professional footballer and a well known member of the community was taken away as soon as I got my first order. I was told to strip off, with my suit, shirt and shoes put in a big heavy box. Just to ensure I got the message, the prison officer added: 'You will not be seeing these for a while.' Next came my first mistake. One look at the shower and I didn't fancy it at all. 'Get in that fucking shower!' the prison officer bellowed. I was being put in my place from the very start. Taking hold of the carbolic soap, I edged onto the stone floor and prepared myself for the inevitable. The water was freezing, totally freezing. I washed gingerly, taking a few moments to take in what was happening. That shower took away the sweet smell of aftershave; I wasn't going to smell that again for a good while. I came out of the shower naked and much colder than I went in. I went to the hatch where I was handed my prison clothes – a blue and white striped shirt, donkey jacket and grey jumper with blue cuffs and a collar – plus a knife, fork and black plastic cup. The fork had been chewed until almost flat.

I was given an odd pair of shoes, a size seven and a five, and handed my bedding all rolled up. Then I was led back into the room before going up to the wing. It was about 9pm. C-wing meant nothing to me, but turned out to be the worst in the whole prison. We were supposed to be locked up 23 hours a day with one hour for 'association', social time in a court area to have a walk or a cigarette. That never happened during my first week. The only time anyone was allowed out was to collect food. When I say food, I mean the prison slop because it was very difficult to work out what it was. I've always been a bit of a picky eater, used to eating in the best restaurants in Sheffield and shopping in Marks and Spencer, so this was a major culture shock. I set eyes on my first meal and decided there and then I couldn't stomach the food in that block.

Mark was put in a different cell on C-wing and I didn't see much of him to be honest. It proved to be a parting of the ways after being friends for a couple of years or so. To be honest, we never discussed what happened in that court room and haven't really spoken since. It wasn't a case of falling out in prison but he went his way and made a few new friends and so did I. I think he held it against me that we'd been more harshly treated because I was a footballer and made a public example of. But that was never said in the open. Neither do I blame Mark for what happened. Who hasn't made a dash for the pub to get a pint before closing time? Who hasn't gone through an amber light at some time or other in their life? Any driver who says they haven't is probably a liar. But going through that traffic light literally changed my life.

I was marched into my cell which was about 12ft by 6ft with a stone floor. Inside was a bunk bed, single bed, table, chair and bucket. Already in the cell was a black guy, probably in his mid-20s, on the single bed and an older guy, I'd guess in his 50s, on the bunk. Neither said a word or even glanced up to me. Mine was the top bunk bed. Nervously, I unravelled my bedding which turned out to be seven pillow cases and nothing else. In panic, I went to the cell door and pressed the button for help. After about 10 minutes, someone finally came to answer. I hadn't got any bedding but was bluntly told: 'You're wasting your time. See you in the morning!'

There was no Perspex in the window and the cell was absolutely freezing. I wrapped the donkey jacket around me as tightly as possible in a bid to keep warm. Soon the light went out and I just laid there, listening to the noises of shouting and screaming from the rest of the wing. In the middle of the night I got to know my cell 'mates'. I woke up to see the black guy pleasuring himself, then the older guy shitting in the bucket before pulling his trousers up and going back to his bunk. The darkest of thoughts went through my tortured mind. How the hell could I get through this?

The cell door was opened at 6.30am for slopping out. I hadn't got anything to get rid of but was made to stand in line with the others as we went to the sluice, emptied the bucket and went back to the cell. The older guy told me: 'Keep out of my way and I'll keep out of yours.' It was just about the only thing either said to me during my week there.

I never had a wash or a shave and when the screw came to give us exercise he just ignored me so I stayed in the cell. I was called down to a room on my first full day. I was sat down at a desk with four officers for company and asked questions. 'Religion?' Catholic, I said. 'Heterosexual or homosexual?' I answered heterosexual but one of the officers stood staring, obviously recognising me as a footballer. 'When you lot score goals, don't you kiss each other? Mark him down as maybe homosexual.'

Told I had visitors, I was handed a bib and made to stand in line. Seeing Mum and Dad there was very difficult yet very precious. I'd let them both down very badly. They brought me up with good, honest, decent values and I'd got myself locked up in a hellhole with the scum of the earth. I saw them looking at the other prisoners. What could they be thinking? It hurt so much to see both so visibly upset. Yet they were fantastic with me. Not for one moment did they quiz me about the circumstances of the case. I was their son. I was at my lowest ebb and they were there to support me. I couldn't have hoped for a better response from the two most important people in my world. I am so lucky to have them.

I didn't eat a thing during that horrible week. When I first joined the food queue, I made the mistake of asking for a serviette. That got me a fair amount of stick for a start. I was more or less feeding my cell mates. I looked at my first meal and decided there and then I couldn't stomach food in that block. I had no choice but to fill my tray up with the rubbish they had to offer – some kind of meat, slushy potato and gravy that looked more like soup. When I got back to my cell, the others helped themselves to my meal. They'd just say 'so are you eating it then?' and tucked in.

That was about as near as I got to talking with them. They kept themselves entirely to themselves, read books, went to bed and used the bucket.

Imagine my relief when the door opened and the officer I met at Sheffield Crown Court repeated he had a job for me and I was leaving C-wing. I couldn't grab my things quickly enough – anywhere had to be better than this place. I was later told B-wing was where I really should have been from the start as this was the home of prisoners who had committed motoring and other comparatively minor offences. There was Perspex in the window – thank God – so it was a little warmer, if still very basic. The officer explained my job was in the tea bar. All things are relative, I suppose, and life was looking up.

After not having a shower or exercise during my time in C-wing, my green band allowed me the luxury of a daily wash, plus I now had a job and was getting paid so I had money to spend in the shop. My new cellmate, Richard, who was inside for motoring convictions, was more human. The guy had been driving for 10 years and banned for 11! Each time he saw a car he pinched it. He looked like a rat, but was actually a pleasant guy – a definite improvement on the occupants of C-wing.

I got up at 6.30am to get ready for work. I cleaned my teeth and reported to the tea bar before the officers came in. I made them tea, beans on toast and cheese on toast. I did three meals instead of two, so I could get something reasonable to eat myself. As long as I stood facing the wall, the officers didn't worry. If I faced them with my cheese and toast, they'd kick off. The price of the meal was £1.50. I dropped £1 in and kept 50p in my hand, something they happily let go.

I quickly learned how things worked. If I was good to the officers, they were good to me. In return for Mars and Twix bars which I took from the tea room where I was working,

I was given a brand new vest and leather lace-up shoes. Everyone knew what I was doing and let me know. One day an officer stood in front of me as I was laden with chocolate bars and the like. My heart was thumping ten to the dozen at the thought of being found out. The screw threatened to give me a good hiding, but then said he was only kidding. I was very relieved. The last thing I wanted was to be sent back to C-wing.

The prison had its own way of dealing with enemy number one – child molesters. One day in the food queue it went like this: an Asian guy, convicted for paedophile offences, held out his plate to be served his peas. He was given just a single pea and ordered to move on. At the potato point, the officer stood shaking his head and didn't give him a morsel. The worst was yet to come. Next an amateur boxer made his feelings totally clear. He slung boiling hot custard all over the Asian who was put in a corner screaming before being led to his cell. Later the boxer lifted me bodily out of a queue for the shop before explaining there was another child molester behind him. Paedophile prisoners ran the gauntlet every day in Armley. When officers discovered one on their wing, they slipped their record and cell number under the door of one of the toughest prisoners at night to ensure they were an immediate target for prison justice.

Working in the tea bar was very helpful as it kept me away from the cell during the day. Everyone was locked up by the time I returned so I was out of the way of the worst prisoners. Prisoners screamed, shouted, even fought and stabbed each other, just part of the daily mayhem that passed for life in Armley.

I didn't get it all my own way as officers in the tea bar brought me down to earth every now and again to show who was boss. But I was very grateful for the cheese on toast and avoiding being poisoned by the other prison food. I could also see the road with cars driving up and down. It was just enough to remind me in bleaker moments that I would be joining them again one day.

After a month, I was transferred to an open prison called Rudgate at Wetherby. I was allowed to apply for a move after about a fortnight at Armley and it was a total no-brainer. I processed all the paperwork as quickly as possible and was told about three or four days in advance that I could serve the rest of my sentence in the category 'C' prison next to the mainstream prison in Wetherby. It was on the minibus to Rudgate that I first set eyes on Chris Ray. A big handsome black guy with long hair in plaits and pearly white teeth, he knew who I was and warmly shook my hand. He'd been in prison for a couple of years after being involved in a drugs operation and also told me he had run a couple of brothels.

The two prisons were as different as chalk and cheese. Rudgate had its share of murderers and armed robbers but was usually for prisoners coming towards the end of their sentences. I knew it was more relaxed from the moment we were led in and presented with our clothes in a box. We were met at the door by a tall gym officer who told me I'd be playing in his football team. 'You must be joking,' I replied. Chris and I were both led into an 18-bed dormitory. I had the bed next to the door, not a good idea because I got the full benefit every time someone came in and banged the door.

Chris had a couple of karate schools and was a bit lethal. Luckily, we quickly became very good friends. He took me under his wing and helped make my stay in the new prison as comfortable as possible. He even stood outside when I had a bath, as if having a proper towel wasn't enough. Chris was my guardian angel for those two and a half months and I'll never forget it.

The gym officer came up with a job as a domestic for me. I told him straight I wasn't going to play in his football team for the privilege of cleaning floors and toilets so he'd have to think of something better. He gave me a job as a gardener, telling me people were nicking stuff and he wanted me to look out for him. That sounded better but, working outside in the freezing cold and rain, I seriously wondered what kind of favour he'd done me. Also, there was no way I was going to get involved in snitching on prisoners.

I had an office visit. There were administrative things to sort out such as finances and the house and my barrister promised to take care of things for me. The visit was from the barrister's secretary to tell me what was happening. The look on her face spoke volumes. The last time I'd seen this smart looking lady I was looking dapper in an Armani suit waiting for the verdict. Now she looked up from her desk at a dishevelled figure in a donkey jacket. It was enough to move her to tears. She asked if there was anything she could get me. 'A coffee and a biscuit,' I replied and she made me a drink.

After our meeting, I was introduced to the gym officer's boss, Mr Ridings, a pocket-rocket in his mid 40s with rippling muscles that almost burst out of his shirt. He'd been in the army and told me in his broad Yorkshire accent that there was a job going as a gym orderly. I would hand out the odd top and shorts and, when all was quiet, get the chance to work out in the gym. Usually two men did the job and one had left. I accepted straightway as this was definitely better than cleaning or gardening.

Mr Ridings was high up in the prison service and we quickly got on very, very well. We were woken up at 6.30am and I prepared things in the gym before breakfast at 8am. It felt like being at a boarding school with prisoners walking around doing their laundry. Mr Ridings told me to meet him outside the gym on a Monday, Wednesday and Friday morning to go for a run along the road outside Wetherby racecourse. He was a fit guy and all was fine as long as I ran behind him. We talked football all the way.

Fellow inmates were told in advance I was coming to Rudgate and, although some backed off thinking I'd be aloof and superior, being a footballer served me very well in there. Prisoners asked me to write letters to wives or girlfriends. As I kept their business quiet, word spread and I was called on more and more. I felt quite touched, as it showed they trusted me. I politely refused their offers of tobacco for doing them a favour.

Another prisoner asked me to cut his hair which I didn't make a very good job of. Each time I tried to level his hair out, the sides were getting shorter and shorter. He never came back! Drugs were rife, as at Armley. Although I wanted no part of it, it intrigued me how they sneaked them into the prison. It was usually through a kiss from their wife or girlfriend. Word got round that a prisoner was waiting for his load before human nature took its course. Mobile phones were also frequently smuggled in whereas I felt sick with worry when a visitor gave me the luxury of four stamps.

Rudgate was a strange old place in so many ways. It looked like a big army camp inside with people walking freely around. This could have been a problem as it meant anyone with a grudge could find you more easily but Chris made sure I was safe and sound. Night times saw some almost comical happenings. Often I saw a hooded figure with a pillow case on his head and the eyes cut out making a dash for it. A car would pull up outside the gates and the prisoner was primed to collect alcohol that would be thrown in. The challenge was to make it back to his cell before the screws caught up with them. They screws must have known what was going on but let them get away with it because it was too much hassle to stop them in the middle of the night. Occasionally, the alcohol run provided us with a bonus as we'd get a can of beer thrown into our cell and enjoy a few welcome sips of the hard stuff between four of us. Rudgate nights also included the luxury of being able to go out to the loo and even make a drink or a cup of soup if struggling to sleep.

I discovered real talents in there with some of the artists being fantastic and the prisoners having all kinds of ingenious ways of making things to try to improve their lot. One practice though made my stomach turn. They caught rabbits and tried to boil them after washing out canisters that had been filled with bleach. They then warmed their catch on radiators in their cell – the mere thought could have put me off food for life!

Lads were more likely to talk with me because I was a footballer. I never asked what they were in for but often on the way to football they opened up with their personal stories. I wondered at first why a guy would steal a TV set or carry out an armed robbery but left thinking 'but for the grace of God go I'. There are bad people in there, for sure, but desperate circumstances led others to go down the wrong path. Crazy actions can never be right but are more understandable when you don't know where the next penny is coming from and are worried sick about your family. After committing one crime, offending becomes easier and easier until it turns into a self-destructive pattern. There were definitely people in there more at ease behind bars than out in the community and I'm not just talking about the tramps who smashed enough windows to get themselves locked up when needing respite from the winter cold.

It all leads me to think politicians talking about rehabilitation are from a different universe. They believe all that is needed is for someone to come and chat to the prisoners, tell them the error of their ways and they will go straight. Sorry, that's bollocks. I met prisoners who felt there would be nothing out there for them once they were released. Coming out with £50 in their pockets and no prospect of a job meant they were likely to turn back to crime to ease their immediate worries. After all, in prison they were guaranteed three 'meals' a day, a roof over their heads and no bills to pay. It's even worse now the same politicians are taking away their benefits. I met people in prison just crying out for someone somewhere to give them a chance – until that happens the cycle will go on and on.

I still wasn't really eating as the food at Rudgate was also disgusting. I was warned by a guy in the kitchen not to eat the fish because of the rat and mouse droppings. There was, however, a vegan among the kitchen staff and I could go on that if I wanted. So I made an appointment and met this portly bloke who explained everything. The first couple of days went really well and I had a meal at last but then it went wrong. I looked at my plate and all I could see was a green mess – it really didn't resemble anything I could recognise. The vegan had gone and the new chef hadn't a clue about vegan food. Again Chris did his best to come to the rescue. As we went down the servery, he asked the officer for a fried egg which I gobbled up as quickly as possible.

Changing my affiliation to Church of England was a good idea, for dietary reasons. Catholic and C of E services were held in the prison with the main difference being you got a Penguin biscuit if you attended the latter. I was losing quite a lot of weight in prison due to hating the food so this didn't do me any harm.

Mr Ridings told me to mark out the football pitch, something I didn't usually have to do as a player! There were four inches of snow outside and the task was virtually impossible. When I protested, he grabbed me by the throat and read the riot act. It was his way of showing that, although we got on well, he was boss. Then coming up to Christmas, I was told to enter the weight lifting competition in the gym. Guys in there were lifting almost Olympic weights and this wasn't really my thing. I kept fit as a footballer but didn't handle too many weights. Mr Ridings gave me a broom handle to practice with which was very amusing for everyone else. More usefully, the other gym orderly left and I told the boss I knew the perfect replacement. Chris getting the job was another boost for my morale.

Chris was also in our football team which played on a nice pitch just outside the prison fence. Officers weren't worried about players escaping. We were told from the start at Rudgate that we knew where the prison exit was – no more than a level crossing anyway – and could leave whenever we wanted. But they guaranteed they would catch us and we wouldn't be coming back to Rudgate. We played football in a league and, although the standard wasn't what I'd been used to, it was quite enjoyable nevertheless. Mr Ridings gave us a half-time pep talk as I sat on the ball, my mind elsewhere.

It was amusing to listen to opponents talking. They were often surprised we weren't such bad lads but didn't know the half of it. We looked like a normal football team on the outside, but were hiding a fair few secrets. Our goalkeeper had split up from his girlfriend, found and attacked the new boyfriend, and killed him. We had a full back who had been inside for 20 years for murder, our main midfielder was an armed robber doing 11 years, and our chief centre forward and goalscorer was also inside for murder. Altogether we sported quite a few lifers towards the end of their sentence.

Mr Ridings took us to the bigger gym to sweep and mop it whilst he had a shower. Instead Chris and I got out a bat, wicket and leather ball and started smashing it to every corner of the gym. Afterwards, the look on Mr Ridings' face was priceless. He said he'd never seen those red marks before but I insisted they'd always been there. He would have killed us had he found out. He also challenged me to a competition for doing most dips, saying he could tie a weight around his waist and still beat me. This wasn't something I was used to, so he was probably right.

With the festive season upon us, Mr Ridings noticed I

still wasn't eating much. Having come off my vegan diet, I had again gone to see the kitchen officer, a strange guy who played the trumpet whilst he was cooking. My Christmas dinner of boiled chicken was so badly cooked that water oozed out as soon as I sank a knife into it. No way was I going to touch that. It was awful. Mr Ridings was worried and found an ingenious way to ensure I didn't go totally without.

I was setting up the gym equipment on Boxing Day when he came in carrying a sandwich in his hand and passed a seemingly innocent remark that his wife had gone and put turkey in it again. He gave the sandwich to me and asked me to eat it there and then as he didn't want anybody else to see what he'd done. I knew exactly what was really happening. He had made the sandwich for me and was making sure I got some food inside me. Bless him, he didn't have to do that. He was a stickler for the rules when others were around – but reminded me that day he had a human side too.

After the football on a Saturday morning, the team was allowed to watch the horse racing. We took odds to make it more interesting and Chris and I set up as bookmakers. The currency was Mars Bars and tobacco rather than money. After most sessions, our cupboard was full to the brim. As a special treat, Mr Riddings arranged for most of the team to go hill walking in the Yorkshire Dales dressed in green. We were approached by two old men in their 70s who politely asked us which regiment we were from. Mr Ridings ordered us to walk on to spare our embarrassment.

I was very popular in prison, far too popular for the liking of the authorities. I got a lot of mail, mostly from people I'd never met. There were 20 or 30 letters a day from Blades fans, something I was very grateful for but which annoyed others. Whilst most prisoners were longing to see their number go up on the board to tell them they had mail, my DFO506 was up there constantly. Many times I went to my bunk to read through the letters, which really keep you going in prison. The thought that these people had gone to the trouble to find out where I was and taken time out to write was very humbling. There was not one single letter having a go. Typically, they said I'd received a harsh sentence and were thinking of me.

Visitors are also very precious and my parents came to see me every week. Wisely, they didn't ask much about what the prison was like but used the hour to keep me up-to-date with what was going on in the 'real' world outside. Another person who made my stay a lot more pleasant was a friend called Linda Smith. People must have thought we were an item but that wasn't the case. Linda had long since been a part of my Sheffield social life as I'd known her since I was about 20. She was another who took the time and effort to write to me very frequently to encourage me that I would get through it. We are still friends today and I'll always be grateful to her for her kindness.

One useful piece of info was that any prisoner who got themselves a job interview, would be let out for a day. My uncle Jack ran his own business so we arranged for him to send a letter saying I had an interview with him. My plan got the green light so Dad took me home to Leeds, a 30-minute drive. I was allowed out first thing in the morning and had to be back by 5pm. Just having a peaceful bath and feeling a warm carpet under my feet reminded me of the apparently trivial things I'd been missing. Knowing I was a footballer also came in useful when the prison officers and governors were arranging a function and wanted some stuff. I wrote to Mel Stirland and Phil Thompson and managed to get some autographed Leeds and Liverpool shirts for the prison which they really appreciated. Uncle Jack then produced another letter about a second interview. The officers knew it was a con but weren't bothered, happily allowing me to spend another day in Leeds.

My mind had been fixed on my release date for some time and the last week was mostly a case of marking time and getting my gear ready for going back into civilisation. There was one more shock before I left when I was handed my own clothes back. Fuck me, I couldn't believe it was my suit; I'd lost two and a half stones inside and they were no longer my size. Nevertheless, I had no choice but to wear them and the hint of after shave more than made up for any slight discomfort. There's a distinct prison smell – carbolic, bleach, sweaty bodies – and I was more than happy to sniff my real life again.

My release time was 7am and Dad, as loyal and reliable as ever, was there about an hour before to pick me up. More surprisingly, Mr Ridings had come to work early on his motorbike, especially to say goodbye to me. He said he'd enjoyed my company and repeated his view that I shouldn't have been there in the first place. It was another great gesture he didn't have to make and left me with another very fond memory.

There weren't a lot of words said between me and Dad on the journey back to Leeds but it was nice to go out to a pub together that evening. His words then are still imprinted on my mind: 'You can't get any lower, son,' he said. 'The only way now is up!' That summed up the support of both my parents. They must have been in terrible mental pain having a son in prison, yet they never once made things any more difficult for me than it already was. From the very start, their attitude was not to concentrate on prison life but look forward to when I could get my life back on track. It was thanks to them as much as anyone that I was able to do just that.

I stayed in Leeds for a week before Linda took me back to Sheffield and a party she'd arranged for my homecoming at the Rising Sun. It was nice of her, as always, but I didn't go. Prison wasn't something I was proud of – just the opposite.

I didn't have any reason to celebrate. I was just beginning to come to terms with the outside world again, and being around people who were intrigued about what I'd been through was the very last thing I wanted. I needed physical and mental space to get my thoughts together and wash the stench of prison from my mind.

Being pursued by the press was another pain. Unfortunately for me, the issue of footballers going to jail was given extra legs by former England skipper, Tony Adams, being sent to Chelmsford Prison for drink driving shortly after my own release. A couple of national newspapers contacted me, wanting me to talk about my experience of prison life so they could reflect what Adams was likely to go through. I wasn't keen on the idea but they told me that, if I didn't co-operate, they would write about me anyway, so it would be in my best interests to ensure the correct story was published. So I decided to tell my story to the *Daily Mirror* and was surprised when it made a double page spread over two successive days, although the main focus was on Adams rather than me.

In the weeks following my freedom I let my hair down socially by partying at the house of Linda and her husband Richard. I'd spent plenty of time there over the years as they had many friends and contacts in Sheffield, but this was something different. I may have missed female company being banged up in prison but more than made up for it in the few weeks that followed. Being a footballer guaranteed I was never short of offers but having a prison label gave me extra spice. Maybe women were attracted by my new bad boy image. They were so brazen, it was frightening. I had young ladies I'd scarcely set eyes on approaching me in a bid to be my 'first'. I admit I played on that over the next three or four weeks, with plenty of women believing they had been successful!

7

Rebuilding My Life and the Brealey Years

REGAINING my freedom was one thing, sorting my life out was quite another. Readjusting to 'normal' life is a massive challenge for any prisoner but my personal dilemma was made more difficult by the fact I'd virtually come to the end of my professional football career.

My six-month contract at Huddersfield was understandably cancelled as a result of my imprisonment. It would have expired by the time I was free anyway. Soon after my release I went to a presentation at Bramall Lane and spoke with Blades manager Dave Bassett. He asked me what I was doing now I was out of prison and I said not a lot. He invited me to come and train at my old club – a gesture I really appreciated. I never played under Harry but his attitude impressed me greatly. I felt he was totally sincere in his offer and a 15-minute chat was long enough to convince me he was a very good man manager in the mould of Harry Redknapp today. I could very easily see why players wanted to play for him and knew the Blades were in particularly good hands. It's difficult to explain exactly why I never took him up on his invitation. It was partly to do with not wanting to go backwards, and I would have felt a bit desperate leaning on Sheffield United Football Club at a vulnerable moment in my life. I knew I needed a new start, I just didn't know what or where it would be.

I needed breathing space away from Sheffield if I possibly could. Although genuinely touched by all the letters of support from local people whilst I was inside, I was worried about the reception I would get now I was back in the community. I was also far from sure how I would handle it myself. I was very embarrassed by what had happened and, despite the article in the *Daily Mirror*, didn't want to be the subject of public attention.

I was very lucky to get an offer out-of-the-blue from a friend called Wesley Smith, whose father ran a construction firm. He invited me to Nottingham to do some tarmacing work for a couple of months alongside Ray Storey who was once on Manchester United's books. The important thing however was that, to them, I was purely 'Tony', not a footballer, or a well-known person.

I hadn't got a clue about the job at first but put my heart and soul into it, getting my hands dirty, enjoying myself, and putting welcome cash in my pocket. More than that, going on the road with Smiths Construction gave me a welcome break at just the right time.

I would have gladly never seen or heard about prison again in my life. But I'd made a promise. Chris was due for release some four or five months after me and I said I'd go and visit him. Even driving back to Rudgate gave me the creeps. But Chris was a great lad, whose company and humour had kept me going, and I got over my discomfort to see him. He told me he wasn't sure how he was getting home to Leeds when he came out, so I told him I'd be there at the gates for him. We didn't keep in touch afterwards but had been good mates when we needed each other most.

I did get another football offer from Chris McMenemy, son of Saints legend Lawrie, who was in charge of Chesterfield.

He told me I could team up again with a friend of mine, John Ryan, the former Wednesday and Newcastle full back I played with at Mansfield. That helped swing it and I enjoyed a short time at Saltergate playing about half-a-dozen reserve games.

There was no problem with my general fitness. My spell in prison with all the gym training and very little food ensured I came out physically as fit as a fiddle and having lost weight. But I couldn't beat Father Time on the injury front. My back was playing up, and I had knee and ankle problems as well. Reluctantly, I had to accept the obvious truth. Total single mindedness, a passion for the game I loved, and being prepared to shelve all the negatives, had got me back onto a football pitch several times against good medical advice, yet I was now weary in mind and body and didn't have the fight to carry on. At 29 years of age I had to look fairly and squarely at what my body was telling me – and consider I still had a lot of life in front of me.

I didn't have a Plan B to fall back on after the end of my football career. I recalled once again being a teenager in the bath at Bramall Lane and those wise words of Geoff Salmons, who told me to enjoy every moment of my playing days because it would be over in a flash. I thought I was invincible and would never have to worry about life outside of football. Of course, he was right. It really had gone so quickly and I had to find another way forward. The issue of what to do after football was never talked about at Bramall Lane. That was the norm. I thought I might be interested in coaching and, like the other United players, had been put through my preliminary badge. So I had a foot on the first rung of the ladder, if you like. However, coaching qualifications were seen very much as secondary to experience or having a big name – and I had neither.

Getting a phone call from my brother Terry in New Zealand was a big break. We'd kept in regular touch through the years, including a spell of about 18 months or so when he returned to live in England. Now his own semi-professional playing career was over and he was working as a measurer for a firm of drapers. I'd never been to New Zealand but when he suggested I get involved with a club over there I had nothing to lose. I actually had two offers as the PFA also contacted me about going to play for a club in Napier, but quickly made my mind up.

I rented out my house in Sheffield to take a look at life on the other side of the world, soon becoming player-coach at a club called Mount Wellington in Auckland and living in Browns Bay near the beach. The club's chairman, Bobby Douglas, who ran a long-standing bakery company called Bakels, had another idea for me. To justify signing and paying me decent money, he asked me to come and work for him during the close season.

This was definitely something completely different. Apart from the short period laying tarmac, the only time I'd worked in the 'real world' was for two weeks when I was about 19 – a move that came about in interesting circumstances. Although not a golfer myself, I spent a fair amount of time socialising at Dore and Totley Golf Club, where I got to know George Ward, a massive Wednesday fan who ran a scissor-making factory. He had a wager that, as a footballer, I couldn't hack it working with him. If I proved him wrong, he'd pay me for the privilege. It wasn't a lot of money but I just wanted to show a mate what I could do. So I reported for work at his factory just outside the town centre and was given my task – drilling holes in scissors. Everyone knew who I was and the banter and mickey-taking flowed from the beginning. But I was useless at the job. The hole had to be drilled first, then the screw put flush on. Unfortunately, I didn't quite follow the instructions and ended up ruining half of their pinking scissors as well as getting burnt by the hot metal.

Male workers on the production line were a bunch of old diamonds who regularly asked what 'this fucker' was doing there. I also ran the gauntlet of female office workers who weren't slow to laugh and let rip with raucous remarks about the young footballer. This was their stomping ground and they were eager to have a go at the whipper-snapper who'd come to join them. Despite getting things wrong, I really enjoyed my fortnight there and was none the worse for the experience. The banter was great, rather like the dressing room. Both can be tough places to be and can teach you a lot about yourself. They help you to develop a second skin to survive because otherwise people find out your weaknesses and attack them.

The question now was could I hack 'real work' 10 years older and wiser but well out of my comfort zone in New Zealand? It was time to find out. My first job was working on the conveyor belt alongside some very beefy Maoris. Basically, the oats and other items came down the conveyor belt and my job was to put these big heavy sacks into cardboard boxes and send them on their way onto the pallet to be forklifted to the warehouse. This was happening at a very fast rate and the Maoris worked furiously to get a bonus for exceeding their target of full pallets. I couldn't prevent loads of sacks falling onto the floor as the Maoris raced down the conveyor belt to try to stack them for me.

After just one day, I was moved into a little room where they made the icing sugar. I was working with a lovely Maori guy called Wayne, whose task was to make and blend the icing sugar and put it into a big tub. My job was to make the box from the flat pack and put it onto the scales. The icing sugar came up to be measured and put into the boxes. I then had to chop the icing sugar with my gloved hand and zip it up. Instead the icing sugar was soon ending up on the floor with Wayne running around like a blue-arsed fly trying to rescue it. I was making his job very difficult but he never moaned once.

Again, I only lasted a day before being switched once more to work on the hopper filling the sacks up. What I wasn't told, however, was that every now and again the hopper would get stuck and needed to be hit with a big broom. Unfortunately, I forgot to secure the bottom of the hopper and the flour came flooding out of the sacks, filling the room with what looked like a fog. You've guessed it – I was moved on next day, this time working with the 3oz sacks full of powder to make the oats for the bread. I was warned never to let the needle on the machine go higher than 50 – or else! I honestly thought I'd found my niche dealing with the sacks but totally forgot to watch the needle. Bad mistake! I allowed it to go all the way round the scale and into the red before the inevitable happened. The whole machine went bang!

I jumped out of my skin – I swear I'd never seen a scene like it in my whole life. It sounded and looked like a bomb had gone off and I'd just created my own piece of factory history. The place had been running like a well-oiled machine for years before I got my hands on it and managed to bust it for the first time ever. The poor chairman was as kind to me as he possibly could be. 'Look, Tony, go home!' he said. Irony was I really enjoyed myself there. The spirit among the Maoris was great and I enjoyed playing cricket with them during break and lunchtimes. But, through no lack of effort and hard work on my part, I was a total disaster.

I loved New Zealand as a place. I was there about 15 months and the relaxed way of life beside the sea and the good nature of the people gave me the lift and break I so badly needed after my traumatic prison experience. Unfortunately, my body wouldn't allow me to thrive on the football field. I hobbled my way through until the end of the season by which time I needed yet another operation – a hole in my right ankle having limited me to just a couple of games for my new club. Terry and the chairman did me a huge favour giving me the chance to make a new start but I couldn't justify staying in the country any longer.

So I returned to England where I bumped into another influential figure from my past who pointed me towards the future. I was at a benefit dinner for Blades defender and personal friend Paul Stancliffe, and on the same table as chairman Reg Brealey who asked me what I was doing. He took a 'but for the grace of God' attitude towards my prison sentence and invited me to come and see him a few days later.

Reg was in the throes of leaving Sheffield United and had a finger in a lot of pies. He spoke with me about wishing to sell pharmaceutical equipment to football clubs – an idea I wasn't interested in being involved in as travelling from Scotland to Brighton didn't appeal too much. Then he introduced me to a project I was far more captivated by. He was looking to get into social services and sell them a scheme whereby he could help youngsters develop life skills – and emerge with a guaranteed job offer. It involved taking them out of their usual environment for a year to places such as Gibraltar and Brunei. It sounded like a great idea. Sure, there'd be big money in it for Reg, but it would also provide a very worthwhile service. He already had the publicity brochures, got an engineering company called AMEC on board, and even bought the beautiful and isolated Knoydart estate in north west Scotland to use as a base.

I decided to take a look for myself and Reg encouraged me to buy a house nearby to prepare for the scheme taking off. That's why I moved to a place called Arisaig, off the west coast of Scotland. It was a beautiful house in a fantastic unspoilt part where you were more likely to see wild deer than cars. It was absolutely unbelievable, perfect in many ways. But one thing was missing – the job itself. Still waiting for things to happen, I started doing some work for the

Scottish FA and Lochinver Harbour Council taking football coaching sessions for youngsters. Meanwhile it became clear that locals around Knoydart, who only numbered about 50, were up in arms about Reg's proposal. They were worried about a beautiful place being raped and pillaged by young people from difficult backgrounds. I could see their view although I was on the other side of the fence waiting and hoping for it all to take place.

Two years down the line and I was still sat there in limbo. I'd bought myself a great house which would have been ideal if I was of retirement age. Instead I was a young man in my early 30s itching for something to get my teeth into. The situation wasn't helped by a surprise visit from a reporter from the *Daily Mirror*. For some reason, they'd tracked me down to the west coast of Scotland and travelled all the way to my door to get me to blab about Reg. The journo said they knew all about me being left out on a limb as the project hadn't got off the ground and wanted my side of the story. I wasn't impressed. All they wanted was a cheap shot at a wealthy businessman. I told the reporter in no uncertain terms to go away, or something similar.

The visit did have one purpose however. It spurred me to get into my car and drive to Reg's Lincolnshire home– a six or seven hour journey – to find out from the horse's mouth what was going on. It was about 7am when I banged on his door and I was let into the property, a stately home befitting of his status, by his wife. Eventually Reg came down and told me honestly he was really struggling to get the project off the ground. I felt more sorry than angry because I was still convinced it was a fantastic idea that had met with strong opposition and his intentions had been honourable in trying to involve me. Reg gave me money he owed me for the time I'd been waiting and told me about another of his business schemes.

He'd responded initially to an appeal from Darlington

manager Billy McEwan, whom I'd known at Sheffield United, to loan the cash-strapped Fourth Division club some cash to prevent them going out of existence. He ended up taking over the ownership of the Quakers and putting a long term colleague, Steve Morgon, in charge of the business side. Having worked with Reg since he was about 16, Morgon knew Reg inside out and was well equipped to run the administrative side of the operation, without being a football man. My job, Reg told me, was to be a link between the manager and the football side and Steve. I never did have a proper title during my stay at Feethams. Some brave souls called me dogsbody.

First step was to get in my car and meet up with Steve. I spoke with him in the offices – or rather portakabins – at Darlington and started to build up an image of a guy who took a lot of stick during his spell with the club. He was far from subtle in the way he tackled issues which was never going to increase his popularity but did more good than harm behind the scenes there. I told Steve I wanted paying £20,000 a year to work for the club and he just laughed. 'You will get what you get,' he replied, hinting strongly that the finances wouldn't allow him to make too many commitments. I decided that, whatever my income, at least I was working again and in an area I was genuinely interested in.

I found Darlington to be a unique football club during my stay there with Steve Morgon the dominant force. He was loud and opinionated but proved right nine times out of ten. The things he did for that football club were unbelievable. He regularly worked very long hours from about 6.30am until 9pm and paid plenty of the club's bills off on his own card as he set about trying to tackle the debt. We were both useful to each other. I knew how things were done on the football side, so gave Steve a helpful steer when the manager or someone else told him to do something. He checked with me and often I told him what was being suggested wasn't par for the course for a football club at all. In turn, when he felt Reg was taking the mickey with his demands, Steve had the business nouse to encourage me to stand my ground.

The club was pretty well set up for a succession of managers who came in and out of the door. We had young forward, Robbie Blake, who went on to play for a number of high profile clubs, defender Sean Gregan, who also had a good career before returning to help the newly-formed Darlington 1883 club, and goalkeeper Mike Pollitt, who played in the Premier League with Wigan Athletic. We were always having financial scrapes however. One occurred in our bid to keep rats out of the portakabins as we were close to the river. I vividly recall Rentokil coming to take our rat traps away because we were behind with our bills and Steve somehow talked the bloke into buying a Darlington season ticket. Say what you like about Steve – and people definitely did – he was a very good and natural salesman.

Finances were always a worry at Darlington, so imagine our excitement when we drew mighty Liverpool at Anfield in the FA Cup. Such a draw is always a big lift for players and supporters to take their minds off the more mundane matters of Fourth Division football by having a day out against one of the most famous clubs in the world. But to administrators, it can be all about a club's survival as it guarantees a share of sizeable gate receipts. This was a potential pay day that could have kept a club like Darlington going for months, if not the whole season. There was one obstacle in the way, however, and that was Rochdale. For we had drawn our second round tie and needed to win the replay to book our jackpot tie. So I came up with an idea. It wasn't that I was pessimistic about our chance of beating Rochdale, more a need for realism. I wanted to turn our replay into a win-win for both clubs by agreeing we would split receipts from the Anfield clash whoever made it through to the next round.

'We can't do that – it's not right,' said Reg, indignantly.

Anyway we ended up going out of the FA Cup yet Darlington got a fat cheque. Reg had thought again about my cheeky suggestion and phoned the Rochdale chairman to clinch the deal. There was nothing illegal or immoral about it – just the type of out-of-the-box thinking you need sometimes when financial odds are stacked against you. Steve was very cute with the financial side too. Cutting our debts was one thing, bringing the bank overdraft down was quite another. 'We always make sure it doesn't get too small in case the bank takes notice and withdraws it,' he said. Again, we weren't doing anything wrong, merely minding our own backs.

Whilst I was with Darlington, Reg made another bid to get the social services project off the ground. We began to go into a young offenders' prison one day a week to coach young people and also planned to run monthly football courses for around 15 or 16 young people.

I got in contact with an old mate of mine, Brian Marwood, who was working for Nike, and he kindly sent us tracksuits and trainers to make up our kit. When we got our first group from social services, however, my initial plans went straight out of the window as four of them were young girls. They were aged from 14 upwards and I knew straightaway they wouldn't be interested in learning purely about football. So I got to work with some of my contacts and came up with a programme that involved a broader life education.

I picked them up at 8.30am each day and dropped them back at 5pm. I was warned I was onto a hiding to nothing with young people who didn't want to attend school and were likely to cause problems. On day one I could see they were a group of very different individuals but over the next four weeks they gradually became a close unit. There were teething problems as you would expect. I provided them all with packed lunches for the day but found that a lot of

Mars bars were going missing. It was almost second nature for some of the lads to steal. So I had a good chat with them and explained that wasn't really stealing at all because the sweets belonged to them in the first place and they got the idea.

We did all sorts of activities during that very special month, from visiting Brendon Ingall's boxing club in Sheffield to horse racing stables and playing cricket. The police also came in to give a friendly chat. I could see from their body language that the young people were lapping it up. After a few days, they were waiting at the door when I arrived in the morning. I was getting through to them and showing they could learn new things and enjoy themselves. These were needy young people without a doubt. The girls, in particular, could see no further ahead than getting pregnant at 16 or 17 to get a council house.

The cruel thing, however, was that at the end of the month I had to hand those young people back as there was no more I could do for them. So much for Reg's initial plan of looking after them for an extended period and having the contacts in place to offer them employment. We also had youngsters from Middlesbrough Social Services coming into the dressing room and taking on the role of apprentices as part of the football club for a short while. Again, this was good for as long as it lasted.

Reg had an idea to extend the scheme further by buying a local Darlington company and making it into a Soccer Dome. Talks were held with the Wigan chairman Dave Whelan, who was very interested in being part of it. It looked as if he was going to set it up under a different name and a fantastic pioneering project would see the light of day. Cost was the obstacle. Reg was a wealthy man, but even he didn't quite have the financial clout to get the scheme moving. It would cost millions to run properly and that kind of finance wasn't on the table. We also ran into the minefield that is the social services making life more and more difficult. There was a feeling that once they saw we were enjoying success with young people, they were worried about their jobs being on the line. This was a red tape battle we were never going to win.

Meanwhile the fact I was a former player was causing problems with the new Darlington manager David Hodgson. For whatever reason – and I swear I never said or did anything – the former Liverpool striker saw me as a threat from the day he came through the door. 'I'm just keeping the manager's seat warm for you,' he told me pointedly. Nothing was further from the truth. I had no ambitions to become Darlington manager and in any case Reg had marked my card. 'You'll never be manager here because I might have to sack you – and I'm not going to do that,' he said.

Hodgson, however, continued to be suspicious of my motives and we were destined never to get on. He had his own agenda for offering me the post of youth team coach. He had overspent on his budget and getting someone inside the club to take the post saved cash. He made it clear he wasn't interested in the young players and probably thought he was diverting me from any first team ambitions by giving me the job.

A very sorry sight greeted me when I took the youth job – rag tag players who didn't even look the part. Darlington apprentices were coming in each day in Sunderland and Newcastle tops. I'm not having a go at them because they hadn't been treated as important members of the football club. Also the first team management didn't go out of their way to ensure we had necessary equipment – including balls. My first job was to instil discipline and pride into these young players to get them to see they could progress if they put their minds and bodies into the task.

The flip side of the fact that nobody else in the football

club could be bothered with the youngsters was that I had a free hand to come up with my own programme. The way those youngsters responded was unbelievable. They started dressing and acting differently and thoroughly enjoyed going into another of the local youth offenders prisons to play football and learn more about life and how lucky they actually were. What's more, they were beginning to play well too. We drew up a schedule of games and gave Doncaster Rovers a good walloping in the first one. It was an incredibly fulfilling experience for me to see lads I was working with doing so well. But it was a sense of achievement that was to be very shortlived.

Hodgson brought in former Middlesbrough colleague Jim Platt as his assistant, having failed to attract Mark Procter. Platt was another character I found very difficult to get on with and I've no doubt he played a part in what happened next. Steve Morgon told me the duo had decided to bring in their own man as youth team coach. Naturally I was disappointed but bit the bullet and went along with their decision. Next day I packed away my tracksuit, put on my suit and went back to the day job on the administration side. The look on their faces told the story. They thought that by relieving me of my youth team duties I was out of the club. Naively, they'd forgotten the fact I was employed by Reg Brealey rather than them and merely reverted to my original post.

The Hodgson-Platt partnership also came to grief. I was at Steve Morgon's house in Sleaford when we got a call to say the manager was resigning. The message came through to expect the assistant's resignation later. However Platt showed what a character he was by going back on his word and instead asked if he could take up the reigns. Somehow we managed to get to the Fourth Division play-offs that season.

I'm being honest when I say that achievement probably

had more to do with the ability of the players than the management. However we were beaten 1-0 by Plymouth, ending our chance of promotion to the Third. Platt gave me a second spell as youth team manager whilst making it plain he had no interest in them himself. Again the equipment was very limited, often being left with just one ball.

It was during this spell I recommended that a very good young player called Paul Robinson should be considered for first team selection. At first, the manager wasn't at all interested. The fact I was doing the recommending wasn't in the young player's favour. Then Steve told Platt we were sending Robinson out on loan to Bishop Auckland and, strangely enough, the manager had him in his first team the following Saturday. Robinson went on to fulfil his promise by playing for Newcastle United.

After Platt had gone, we knew Hodgson was interested in returning to take up the vacant manager's post. Although I didn't get on with him, I agreed for purely football reasons that we should have him back. Hodgson wrote in his book that I had deliberately ignored him on his first day. Truth was I didn't see him but I would have ignored him. I expected him to at least have the common decency to take me aside at some stage and explain the problem. But he never did. His actions made it quite clear he didn't want to know me. He probably thought that, with me in the way, he wouldn't slip much past Steve Morgon. He was definitely right on that score!

*****

It was during my time at Darlington that I hit the jackpot in my personal life as I met my future wife Jacqueline. Predictably there was a football link to it and the way my bachelor days came to an end wasn't exactly conventional. We'd taken on a young player called Peter Kirkham, recommended by the same scout who discovered Paul Gascoigne. That wasn't the only thing he had in common with Gazza, as he was also one of the most naturally talented players I saw. The way he could juggle a football was mindblowing and he also just happened to be one of the nicest lads you could wish to meet. He took part very enthusiastically in our social services scheme and also came with Reg and me when we went to Gibraltar to do some coaching. But it was his social contacts that really changed my life. He was going out with a young woman from Stockton and asked me to go out for a drink with them with the promise that she was also bringing one of her female friends with her. That was the good news. The not-so-good news was that this mystery woman was coming with her boyfriend.

I got on well with Jacqueline straightaway and got the impression she might be interested in me too. I made my move when the two girls went to Spain for a week. His girlfriend was in on the masterplan. Peter and I were due to fly out to spend time with them and she let us in on where and when they were going out in Magaluf.

Tickets were bought but Darlo's progress to the play off final at Wembley meant Peter had to change his plans at the last moment. So I'd be flying out there on my own to surprise a woman I'd only met once before. I was very unsure whether I should go. The uncertainty went on literally to the very last minute when I suddenly rang a taxi and got to the airport just in time for the plane. Peter's girlfriend wasn't very impressed he wasn't there but the next two or three days went well between me and Jacqueline, who told her boyfriend it was all over between them when she got back to England.

We then started seeing each other and the rest, as they say, is history. We got married in 1998 at Yarm, a village near Stockton, where Jacqueline was based. It took until I was 38 years old to find the right woman but the timing was good. I was also away from Sheffield and more than ready to make a fresh start as we set up home in Stockton-on-Tees, where we still live today.

At one stage, Reg wanted to wash his hands of the club and actually sold it in a strange deal to a businessman called Michael Peden. It was agreed that Peden should pay Reg in monthly instalments, which rang some alarm bells from the very beginning. Anyway, he started to miss payments and Reg ended up taking back the ownership and sending Steve Morgan and myself back in there to run it for him. Eventually Reg sold the club to local businessman George Reynolds, spelling the end for Steve Morgan and me as we were Brealey's men and wouldn't be needed in the new regime.

As I've said, there were plenty of ups and downs on the Darlington rollercoaster but overall I really enjoyed the experience. It gave me the chance to work on the other side of a football club and see how it is run after being a player for so long. You do begin to see things from a different point of view. It's completely unfair to say – as many Darlington fans thought – that Reg took over to asset strip the club. For one thing, there weren't many assets to strip and people soon forget that the club was going to the wall before Reg bought it.

Our public image wasn't helped one jot by Hodgson who had several opportunities to set the record straight. He may have been a good manager but hung Steve Morgan out to dry, helping make him the scapegoat for all the club's on-field problems. But being in a prime position to know what was really going on, I know Morgan did a remarkable job at Feethams. He performed minor miracles just to keep things ticking over after inheriting a mess and sacrificed time and even his own money to help the club out. I can understand why those things aren't necessarily seen or appreciated by supporters whose only concern is winning football matches and going up the Football League table.

Darlington Football Club could only ever hope to reach a certain level – the Third Division was our Premier League – and purely to keep going we were always going to be a selling club. That meant frustration for fans who could see the potential in our ranks and wanted us to hang on to our promising young players. But when it's a choice between doing so and keeping the club going, you have to be realistic.

Some really good players came through the ranks during that time including Gregan, Blake, Robinson, Pollitt and James Coppinger. Their potential was obvious but we didn't move them on to spite the club. Unfortunately, such rich young talent was always going to look beyond Darlington, as shown by the fact that all went on to have good careers at a higher level.

Don't get me wrong, Reg, Steve and I would have given anything to build a side around that little lot and make the team more successful on the pitch. But we didn't have a hope in hell of financing it. Hodgson had plenty of opportunities to tell the fans and the media the real state of affairs. Instead he played the part of the scorned manager whose efforts to build a successful Darlington side weren't being backed by the staff.

Reg's next move took me into a new area of football. It was a surprise when he announced he had bought Grantham Town, who were in the Dr Martens League Premier Division. This was the first time in my career I'd been involved in non-league football but that didn't worry me once Reg had sold the project. The Gingerbreads were handily placed just one division away from the Conference, non-league's elite, and Reg had a plan to transform the Lincolnshire club by forming a partnership with either a Football League or Scottish League club.

The idea was that Grantham would become a feeder club and get the benefit of giving first team experience to young players coming through the ranks. Clubs such as

Hull City and Notts County, along with Greenock Morton and St Mirren north of the border, were all cited by Reg as real possibilities. But we couldn't get any further than that. Reg's vision was a good one but, as with his noble plans to help young people a few years earlier, he wasn't able to put them into effect all by himself. He needed others to catch the same vision and play ball and it just didn't happen. Then he was left to come up with a Plan B after already putting a fair few eggs into the basket.

He turned Grantham Town into a full-time club with my good friend Danny Bergara taking over as first team manager and his trusted team of Morgon and Kenworthy again running things behind the scenes. Danny also brought in Dave Gilbert, an excellent full back with West Bromwich Albion and Lincoln City, as his assistant and player-coach.

I knew Danny as a terrific coach at Sheffield United, An eccentric, admittedly, but full of ideas and great at getting on with the players. The Danny Bergara I worked with at Grantham Town was just a shadow of that man however. It was a case, I think, of more miles on his personal clock. The shelf life of a football manager or coach is usually limited because it involves so much stress and long hours and most people burn themselves out at some point or other. We saw that with Harry Haslam, Bergara's mentor at Bramall Lane, and now it had happened to Bergara himself.

Results in the early weeks of the season were mixed and Danny resigned to move upstairs – these days you'd call him the Director of Football, I suppose. Reg asked me to become manager about 10 games or so into the season and I snapped his hands off. Most footballers wonder what managing a side would be like and this was my chance. I then put my heart and soul into Grantham Football Club over the next few months. I was already working full time and took the anti social hours and inconvenience on the chin. I had a room at a place called Warmington Hall and lived there during the week before going back to my wife and the family home in Stockton-on-Tees after the match on the Saturday. I then drove back to Lincolnshire next day, ready for a prompt start on Monday morning. It wasn't ideal in many ways but the type of thing managers often do as it's almost impossible to do the job justice without working long, hard hours.

It seemed to be paying off results-wise, at first, but there was a warning of things to come after Morgon told me Reg had just bought Hull. The feeder idea was on and he was to drive to Boothferry Park next day for talks. Then, without further explanation and with Steve on his way, Reg called to say the deal was off. Steve was steaming mad and it was easy to see why. He'd uprooted to buy a house in Grantham, expecting the project to get off the ground but could see the cracks appearing. He also gave me a timely warning after Reg and a couple of other Grantham officials reacted instantly to a thumping good victory at Garry Birtles' Gresley Rovers.

We tore the home side apart that afternoon and were moving quickly up the table, so the trio offered me a really good contract on attractive terms, even including 25 per cent of sell-on fees. Steve made it clear the club couldn't afford it because they were already losing money. So I left the contract unsigned and continued as I was. It was a major blow, however, when Steve decided enough was enough and left his job. He told me Reg owed him money and asked me to speak out against him. I didn't disbelieve the guy after all we'd gone through together but I was in no position to do as he wanted. We've never spoken since, which is very sad, as we worked well together and became good friends.

We may not have achieved feeder club status but I did get great support from a couple of Football League clubs to boost our squad. Barry Fry at Peterborough did us a particularly good turn when I enquired about Chris Cleaver, a young striker I'd been impressed with. Barry was happy to help and also told me he had a promising midfielder called Jerome Samuels who needed first team football.

I knew players at that level would improve our team and when I explained we were operating on a tight budget, he didn't charge us a penny as Posh continued to pay the wages of both players during their loans at Grantham. Notts County boss Sam Allardyce also did us a good turn by lending us striker Mark Quayle.

With the new additions playing well, we reached the lofty heights of second place around Christmas before I saw a side of management I didn't like after the return match against Gresley Rovers. Again we gave them a good beating with Quayle and Cleaver in particularly good form. Birtles came into my office after the match for a drink in a very glum mood. He was convinced he was on the verge of the sack, a prospect confirmed when the Gresley chairman asked if he could use a room to have a chat with his manager. I told him I didn't want any part of it and he needed to do his business elsewhere. I found it sad to see a great player like Birtles treated that way.

Many times since I've seen or read about big names biting the dust at non-League clubs and not being treated with the respect they deserve. How did Gresley Rovers expect to find a better man to run their first team than Garry Birtles, winner of two European Cup medals at Nottingham Forest? I still bump into Garry from time to time when he is covering Premier Division games for Sky Sports and he is now doing a fantastic job as a broadcaster. He's much better off staying in touch with the game that way, in my opinion, than being a manager.

Worse was to follow as my job turned sour just when I thought we might be going somewhere. The first team coach said the players hadn't been paid, which was news to me, even though I hadn't received my wages since Christmas. This was an issue I needed to take up with the owner straightaway. I told Reg it was going to be near impossible to continue to get the best out of the lads if they weren't getting the cash they were entitled to. This was the start of a series of discussions and arguments with Reg as our previously good relationship was put under pressure.

I understood his point of view. He was losing money at Grantham at a time when his businesses weren't doing as well as usual and that couldn't continue indefinitely. I've got no doubt that if he had shed-loads of cash available he would have paid the players, but that wasn't much help in my plight. In that situation, players will walk out sooner rather than later and it's difficult to blame them. When I confronted him with that thought, Reg's reaction disappointed me and told me all I needed to know. He basically said that if players left, I should get some more!

From that moment, I knew I was up against it as manager, yet continued to do my best despite not being paid. At times like that you discover a lot about people and I've got to say Grantham's players did me proud by putting in the effort they did. I faced up to a lot of meetings about the cash issue with lads who probably didn't realise I was in the same financial boat. I negotiated settlements for players at the end of the season which came to less than half of what they were owed, but was the best offer they were going to get in the circumstances. There was nothing much I could do, however, to prevent results from going into freefall and suddenly we were looking anxiously over our shoulders at the possibility of relegation. That was bad business in Reg's eyes. He told me he'd already decided to sell up at the end of the season but would have a much better chance of striking a deal if we were still a Premier Division club. My remit was to do anything I could to keep us up.

We crossed swords a few times after that over players. Some of our better lads were in demand and Reg was clearly angry when I agreed to let Neil Glasser join Nigel

Clough's Burton Albion without asking for a fee. I could see where Reg was coming from – his priority was to get back anything he could to compensate for the losses suffered but I didn't think he was in a good position to do so. The players were no longer being paid by the football club therefore, in my opinion, their contracts were meaningless. I couldn't really stand in the way of anyone who wanted out in those circumstances.

Dave Gilbert, who to all intents and purposes was working with me as a joint manager, also knew where the club was heading – down and quickly! I needed to make a decision. Jacqueline was heavily pregnant with our first child Sofie and I couldn't continue much longer living away from home, putting long hours into a job for which I wasn't being paid. I'm not a quitter by nature but couldn't see any future in the position I'd been placed in and therefore resigned as manager at the end of the season after we'd successfully secured Premier Division survival.

It was a very disappointing end to my first tilt at football management and, to be honest, did a great deal to put me off the job. Dave, a terrific bloke to work with as well as a very good player, took over as manager but wasn't given long enough to turn things around the following season in difficult circumstances. When you see that kind of thing happen to guys steeped in football knowledge, it makes you seriously wonder if it's all worthwhile.

Leaving Grantham Town left me again wondering what to do next. I still had hopes that the social services project, which we'd revived on a smaller scale, thanks to Steve Morgon's hard work whilst at the Lincolnshire club, could take off. But realistically that wasn't something I could rely on.

I also thought of ideas like selling cars or setting up my own small business. The reality was that after years with Reg that were far from perfect but never boring, I was twiddling my thumbs. This wasn't a feeling I liked and, with my new family responsibilities, I owed it to Jacqueline to find something more permanent.

It didn't take long for Reg to come back on the phone with yet another project. He told me he thought he'd bought Chester City and wanted me as manager. Soon afterwards he was talking about getting hold of either Morton or St Mirren and giving me a role there, with Paul Hart being his first choice of manager. I may have been tempted before the Grantham nightmare but this was a case of once, maybe twice, bitten. The worries of working for an unstable football club had given me sleepless nights and turned me off football management. I didn't want to be floating from club to club every year or so, firefighting one crisis after another. Jacqueline, who put up with quite a lot during my spell at Grantham, also gave me sound advice. She wasn't standing in my way but asked whether I honestly wanted to risk going through the same unhappy experience again.

Hand on heart, I couldn't be sure Reg's latest project was any more concrete than his idea of helping young people a few years previously or turning Grantham into a Football League club. Like Danny Bergara, I think Reg's better days were behind him and his actions had an air of desperation rather than meticulous planning. He was a fantastic Sheffield United chairman at his sharpest, but now I doubted whether he could make his dreams come true. So I told him I wasn't interested in managing any of the clubs he mentioned and that was curtains as far as our business association was concerned.

It wouldn't be fair, however, to dismiss Reg like that. I was very grateful to the man for all he did for me and the football club I love. I remember all too well the state the Blades were in when he took over as chairman from John Hassell. We'd just been relegated to Division Four and were literally going to the wall. Never mind, last man out turn off the lights, they were actually taking out bulbs to cut costs during those bleak days – and I'm not joking. Then Reg swept in as bright as a button and set us on an upward path again. Not only did he inject finance, but he also brought in new ideas and an excellent new manager in Ian Porterfield. Reg's mistake, if any, was to stay too long at Bramall Lane. Had he left when we'd just been promoted back to the top flight, he ought to have been carried off the field and had a stand named after him. He did that much for the Blades. Instead he got stick for selling the likes of Brian Deane and co as things again started to turn sour. Reg always had good intentions – whether it was for the Blades, his brilliant idea of linking disadvantaged young people to the football club – something almost all clubs do now as almost second nature – then at Darlington and Grantham Town.

He was known to be mega rich when he took over at Sheffield United but ultimately didn't quite have the financial clout to allow all his plans to become reality. The social services idea, for example, would have needed very large financing to get properly off the ground and, as with all such projects, the rewards would have come further down the line. We envisaged having a conveyor belt of young folk, 15 at a time, receiving life skills training before going off to the likes of India and Brunei to be schooled there and be guaranteed a job at the end of their year. Major companies welcomed the project with open arms because they wanted to be seen to be putting something back into the community. The money it would have brought in, along with the social benefits, would have been massive. Guess it just wasn't meant to be.

8

Life After the Final Whistle

Part One: Football

ASK any former footballer and they'll almost certainly tell you the same thing – we'd all love to roll back the years and get back on that pitch all over again. Count me in as far as that sentiment is concerned. I'm not being a green-eyed monster craving the amazing financial rewards in the game today, I'm just speaking the honest truth. I have a great life right now, in many ways happier and more contented than ever, yet I'd jump at the opportunity of playing the game that gave me so much enjoyment and good memories all over again.

I'm still very much involved in football, I'm pleased to say. The Professional Footballers Association got in touch a few years ago looking for more former players to help them with Press Association work covering football matches. This is how a lot of today's statistics are produced. I was soon being sent out to various grounds, both in the North East and in Scotland, with the task of doing a 90-minute telephone 'commentary'. But this is no ordinary broadcast, as on radio or TV, for I'm in direct contact only with a member of the PA staff at Howden, Yorkshire, who turns my information into a blow-by-blow summary, including possession, shots on and off target, corners, free kicks and stats on how each individual player has performed.

It's quite a sight in those offices on a Saturday afternoon and other match days as the operators are penned in like battery hens. This is one way in which we meet the demand for the almost unquenchable thirst for facts and figures in today's football. It began for me as a good way of getting out of the house, keeping my brain ticking over, and staying in touch with the game I love. A weekly exercise at first, it is now more often two or three.

During the 2012/13 season, I spent a lot of time watching my local Blue Square Premier League side Gateshead in action during their 'home' games. But, as the International Stadium was out of action for some of that time, this meant travelling to various grounds throughout the region. I also get to see a fair amount of Hartlepool who have just been relegated to League Two, and more occasionally, Middlesbrough, whose challenge for promotion back to the Premier League hit the rocks after Christmas.

The PA plays a large part in my working life today as I also took on a role as a SP retainer covering greyhound meetings in 2006 and am still actively involved going to Newcastle and Sunderland stadiums five days a week to keep betting shops bang up-to-date with the very latest odds. I work for an organisation called SIS (Satellite Information Services) and thoroughly enjoy being in a different kind of sporting environment. Once we got over the initial reservations of officials, I was deeply indebted to the likes of Michael Connor, from Ladbrokes, and Kevin Blair and Stuart Macintyre, colleagues at SIS, for taking me under their wings and explaining what the job was all about. I meet plenty of really good people, enjoy the sport and lively banter, and get paid for it.

Meanwhile another string to my football bow is working for Premier League Productions on match days. This gives me close access to top flight football and has enabled me to introduce my son Wil to many of today's stars. He has a collection of shirts, autographs and other mementos other lads of his age can only dream of. My role is to act as a link between the media covering the action and the players. I have an access-all-areas pass and usually spend the game in the tunnel area and near the dugouts. I'm the man who finds out the exact word on substitutions, injuries and other incidents taking place on the pitch. Then I feed that information to the Sky commentators to ensure they know as much as possible about what is happening out of their immediate sight.

Sometimes you'll be listening to Martin Tyler, or whoever is covering the match with his expert summariser, and they'll be speculating about a change that may take place. What you don't know is that someone such as me has just tipped them off that a substitution has already been arranged. I also help the media line up interviews after the match. Almost as soon as the final whistle is sounded, I approach one of the key players and ask him to give the TV boys a few words – being a former footballer breaks down a fair few barriers.

Being a very honest guy got me into a very early scrape in this job after what became a notorious Premier League clash between Newcastle United and Aston Villa at St James' Park back in April 2005. What everyone could see was that Newcastle players Lee Bowyer and Kieron Dyer exchanged blows in the middle of the pitch and were sent off in disgrace during Villa's 3-0 victory. What they may never have got to know, save for the fact that I was there and witnessed it, was that the on-pitch brawl was far from the end of the matter.

Manager Graeme Souness and fellow Newcastle officials did their best to put a lid on a very embarrassing incident by appearing alongside Bowyer and Dyer afterwards in an attempt to get them to apologise to each other. But I'd seen the fight continue in the tunnel after they'd been dismissed.

Being green and very new to the job, I reported exactly what I saw, not knowing what the full consequences would be.

Sky had my word about the off-pitch brawl but Newcastle were insisting the incident hadn't happened. The TV station was desperate to check out a story that was bound to become very big news should they broadcast it. I either had to back down or confirm what I'd already reported. That wasn't really an issue, to be honest. I told Sky that, yes, there had been a further fight between the two players. As soon as the report went out, every media organisation wanted a piece of the action and my mobile phone didn't stop ringing for several days afterwards. When I say I was naive, I hadn't thought through what was likely to happen once I'd passed the report on. It didn't make my life as a then rookie media man any easier for a while at St James' Park, but I'm satisfied I did the right thing and would act in exactly the same way again if I see anything similarly newsworthy in future.

Both roles keep me well in touch with the modern day game, with its many improvements and issues that I really struggle with. I had hoped to be writing this as I was celebrating the Blades clinching promotion back to the Championship at the end of the 2012/13 season but sadly that wasn't to be. Instead I've just been watching the Blades getting knocked out of the League One play-offs by Yeovil, meaning we are now in the third flight for a third successive season.

To make things still worse, it was a disappointingly lacklustre performance to put a cap on a long season that promised much but fell short when it really mattered. I watched the crucial game, our seventh play-off failure out of seven, with my son Wil who witnessed my suffering, the same pain every true football fan knows all too well.

I would have loved to have been in that dressing room to find out whether it hit them in the same way. Going back to my day and the disappointments we regularly suffered, I felt totally gutted for weeks afterwards back then and guilty about slipping away to the beach when we hadn't done our jobs and fellow fans were having the mickey ripped out of them throughout the summer for our failures.

It hurts the staff too, as particularly in these tough financial times, jobs are inevitably on the line when a big club is underachieving in a lower division. Believe me, it's gut-wrenching when you see people you know and respect with their heads down, trying their best to keep out of the firing line. They can get the bullet even though they've not done anything wrong themselves.

Everyone knows it but loyalty is almost extinct in football now and the most important people, the fans, are badly short-changed for the real sacrifices they make to support their team. I'm not having a dig at the Blades players because from what I saw of them earlier in the season they seemed a determined bunch. I'll forgive anyone for being not quite good enough as long as they have given their all on the pitch.

But where they, the managers and even the chairmen, depart from true fans is that they all too often move on seeking the best deal, whilst being a supporter is a job for life. What really winds me up is hearing managers or players speak of their love for a football club and, in particular, footballers kissing a badge they've worn for a short time, then going somewhere else and doing exactly the same thing. They need to have more respect for the fans. Looking Blades players in the eye after the Yeovil defeat would have told me whether they shared my pain or were looking forward to their holidays.

I still believe, hand on heart, that Sheffield United are a Premier League football club. We've got top class facilities, fantastic support and great tradition. We come from a brilliant sporting city that should have a club at the highest level – and that's the Blades, not Sheffield Wednesday! I only have to walk back 'home' and fill my nostrils with a sense of the place to know I'm at a top club. Speaking to my old pal Tony Currie, who has spent years as the club's ambassador and is a Blade through and through, we share that same thought.

Whenever I go to Bramall Lane and meet up with my former colleagues, I think back to days when United were in the old First Division. I see TC scoring that great goal against West Ham United – 'a quality goal by a quality player' – and remember when we missed out on a place in Europe by a handful of points. Then I go through my rollercoaster ride from the First to the Fourth Division and back to the Second and remember just a few of the incidents that shaped my Bramall Lane journey.

I was disappointed by the manner of my departure but that is now long since behind me. The welcome that the club gives to me and the rest of the Kenworthy family whenever we visit Bramall Lane is fantastic. My wife Jacqueline is no football fan and never saw my playing days, but she enjoys the way I am treated. It makes her chuckle quietly, to be honest, to see how people remember the days about which I've been writing, as if they were yesterday.

That is one of the most rewarding reasons for going back there, as far as I'm concerned. I often see the likes of Tony Currie and Len Badger doing corporate work. They tell the supporters there's another former player joining them that particular day and I'll mix with guests in the sponsors' boxes and then be invited onto a stage to make a short talk. Such days still fill me with fantastic memories.

A couple of managers have managed to get us back to the top flight since I left, only for both to be dogged by a dramatic last day relegation. Dave Bassett gets my personal nod over Neil Warnock as the boss I rate highest and would definitely have preferred to play for. As I've already recalled, I came across the former Crazy Gang manager at the end of my career at a function for Paul Stancliffe and was very impressed with his positive attitude towards me. He came across as a warm, approachable guy, the type a player would be more than happy to go out onto the pitch and bust a gut for.

Warnock, on the other hand, has never quite convinced me. Results-wise you can't argue that he obviously knows his job and he did well to take the Blades from a point when we were struggling both on and off the pitch and restore us briefly to the Premier League. However, I'm not sure he's the hard man he likes everyone to think he is. He certainly wouldn't have frightened me with any of his antics.

It was exciting to see the club compete among the very best in the land six years ago but so disappointing it finished as it did. It looked as if we had enough points in the bag with half-a-dozen or so games left before a Carlos Tevez-inspired West Ham started to close the gap. In the end we got ourselves involved in a major argument about the Argentinian and whether he should have been eligible to play for the Hammers. The fact was we didn't finish the job when our destiny was in our own hands as we went down 2-1 to Wigan Athletic at Bramall Lane on the final Sunday afternoon, just as Bassett's team fell in the last seconds of the season at Chelsea all those years earlier. On both occasions, the drama at the death masked the obvious fact that, like it or not, over 38 games we weren't quite good enough.

Our problems under Warnock stemmed from failing to strengthen our team sufficiently when we got up there. We could argue about finances forever but perhaps the club didn't really believe we belonged among the elite. That's not unique to us. The same challenge faces Championship clubs every year. Cardiff City, Hull City and Crystal Palace have just been celebrating their promotions to the Premier League and no one can deny them their moments of joy. But they, too, faced the immediate challenge of having to put together very different squads over the summer to have any realistic chance of survival.

What happened to the Blades in the seasons since is also all too common. It's very easy once you've been relegated to end up going down again – as Wolves have just proved with their fall from the Premier League to League One in successive seasons. Again and again we have suffered from selling our best players and not replacing them. I don't really know Kevin Blackwell as a person, but I'm no great fan of goalkeeper managers and things didn't work out for him either after he'd taken us to yet another play off defeat against Burnley at Wembley in his first season.

The biggest losses were probably Kyle Walker and Kyle Naughton, both to Tottenham Hotspur. Of course, I can understand players wanting to play at the highest level but it's really disappointing that they and others didn't think they could do so by staying with the Blades. It was much the same story when Matthew Lowton went to Aston Villa. In my view, Sheffield United is at least as big a club as Villa but we lost out on yet another highly talented player.

When Blackwell was dismissed we turned to the tragic Gary Speed, who had a short and disappointing spell in the hot seat before taking the Wales job, then Mickey Adams wasn't able to save a sinking ship. So we made yet another change and in came Danny Wilson after previously being with local rivals Wednesday and Barnsley.

The 2011/12 season proved another frustrating one for my club as, after holding what looked like being a decisive lead over close rivals Sheffield Wednesday, we saw our season crumble in the home straight after leading scorer Ched Evans was sent to prison. That was a body blow to floor many a dressing room and almost certainly the difference between us gaining automatic promotion and ending up in the play offs. Owner Kevin McCabe, who I have loads of respect for, kindly invited me to the Wembley final against

Huddersfield Town. Unfortunately, I wasn't able to take him up on that but suffered as badly as any Blade at the home of English football that afternoon as I listened to the penalty shootout on my car radio.

That could so easily have led to the team struggling last season as so often happens after missing out at the final hurdle. But I think the manager proved his worth once again. I know supporters get frustrated when they see the lads not quite putting away smaller clubs as happened in the second half of a very tight season. But from what I witnessed, Danny Wilson had a very clear view of what he wanted from the players and had put sensible systems in place behind the scenes.

I was also a big fan of his back-up team including Frank Barlow and Billy Dearden, men with Sheffield United in their souls. These guys would have let the young players know about the tradition of this great club and what it means to pull on a red and white shirt. There was no doubt in my mind that Danny had a good, honest bunch of players in that dressing room who were pulling in the right direction. Lads such as Colin Doyle and Harry Maguire, a defender who can go as far in the game as he wishes, are my kind of footballers and they impressed me whenever I saw them.

Danny was forced to sell more of our best players, including leading scorer Neil Blackman to Reading at a very important time of the season. No doubt an agent turned his head towards a Premier League club, albeit one that was always likely to be relegated. So he swapped a regular first team place and the chance to score goals with us for sitting on the sidelines as Reading went down. Was the move really in anyone's best interest apart from his agent? Remember, they are always urging their clients to accept lucrative deals because that's the way they get paid most. The player's development isn't really a consideration.

It was still a shock to my system when, with just a handful

of matches still to play, Blades decided to sack the manager and dispense with his management team. I must admit I was so angry I almost picked up the phone to ring the club and ask the question 'why?' As far as I'm concerned, the fans didn't get a proper answer. I genuinely wonder whether clubs change bosses purely to try to get that instant lift that so often comes from having a new man in charge.

It is human nature for players to try to impress a new manager, although that doesn't apply so easily when a club turns, as Blades did, to a caretaker boss already on the club staff. I have nothing at all against Chris Morgan who took over the reigns from Wilson. I've no doubt that, as a player, Morgan was my kind of guy – someone I'd have certainly enjoyed playing alongside. My only concern was that I expected him, as a former defender, to have his back four organised and in good shape for the end of the season instead of looking as poor as we did against Yeovil. As my story has shown, however, fortunes in football can change very quickly and, hopefully, it will be third time lucky for the Blades under new boss David Weir in 2013/14 and we can get ourselves back into the Championship.

What Sheffield United, like all football clubs, need this year, and in the seasons ahead, is stability. People talk about it endlessly and the issue has just been brought up yet again as Sir Alex Ferguson made his exit after 26 magnificent years at Manchester United. But, if we are going to bring this ridiculous managerial merry-go-round to an end, we're going to need to recognise that players are more responsible for a club's success and failure than they are given credit for.

Naturally, the manager has an important influence, I'm not arguing with that at all. But the vast majority of the responsibility rests with men out there on the field. The best manager in the world can put in place all the right preparations but there isn't a whole lot he can do once the players cross that white line. Fans love to see a manager showing passion, barking out instructions and showing the right body language, but I can tell you from very good experience that players don't take a lot of notice during the heat of battle. To be quite honest, I always had enough on my plate concentrating on what was going on around me and not allowing that focus to waver for a second to pay attention to what was happening on the touchline. I often used the excuse that I couldn't hear the manager's voice above the crowd and that was often the case. But, in truth, I wasn't really listening and I'm sure that's the same for footballers today.

The fact that the average lifespan of a professional manager in this country is a mere 14 months is sheer madness. It takes a fair amount of time for a boss to get his ideas across and implement his systems and I'd say seven or eight years is a more sensible length of stay unless he is simply not up to the job. Everyone speaks in reverential terms about Sir Alex and Arsene Wenger being at great clubs such as Manchester United and Arsenal for such a long time, yet it doesn't seem that other clubs have the courage and patience to copy their good example. Continually bringing in new managers turns a football club upside down and creates uncertainty. Yet chairmen fall for the three card trick almost every time a club goes through a bad patch. The result is that player power goes through the roof – they're already paid more than the guy who is supposedly in charge of them, now they know there's every chance of getting rid of him if it's seen that he has 'lost the dressing room'.

When I fell out with Martin Peters, I had every reason to think it would be my head, not his, on the block. There was only one winner in any such confrontation and that was always going to be the manager. I would have been out of Bramall Lane but for the manager's departure that summer which I had no earthly inkling of. But now players know that the boss is on borrowed time and there's nothing a manager can do if the players aren't putting in 100 per cent for him. So the manager gets the sack and players sit on lucrative contracts making the job harder for whoever comes next. Perhaps it's because of the constant scrutiny of football clubs by the media and on fans' forums that chairmen feel obliged to change course so often. It's difficult to see this trend changing any time soon, to be honest.

Having the privileged view of Premier League football today through my Premier League Productions work gives me an inside track on worrying trends – and I actually fear for the futures of some of today's top stars. They are playing the game they say they love but you hardly ever see them smile. They're multi-millionaires yet some don't even put in a decent 90-minute shift. The world should be at their feet yet every Tom, Dick and Harry has a camera phone and they are always just one false step away from shock newspaper headlines. Do I envy today's footballers? Not really, to be quite honest. The way they are spoiled at the top level, in particular, means they're storing up trouble for themselves after they finish playing.

Not only are they paid the earth, but clubs look after every fine detail down to dental appointments and looking after their passports to ensure they can focus fully on playing. They just click their fingers and issues that ordinary folk have to sort out for themselves are done for them. They get things their own way so easily, some probably don't know the meaning of the word no. They are so pampered it's pathetic. That's why some behave like brats on the field – they think all they've got to do is put their hands up and yell and a referee is going to do what they want as well.

My era was filled with players, including myself, who had to think very, very hard what we were going to do once we left football behind. Yes, I was paid very well as a footballer but I still had most of my life in front of me and needed, for my own satisfaction as well as financially, to find another path. Today's multi-millionaires living in mansions will think first about going into management or coaching or the media, but there'll only be so many jobs in football to spread around. So, instead, many will disappear into their ivory towers and never be seen again.

Believe me, we are going to hear more and more stories of depression and mental illness among footballers because even having all the luxuries isn't going to be enough. It doesn't matter whether you have £50 or £50m if you are clanging around a big house with nothing to do, no real aim in life, and not knowing how to relate to people you have become isolated from for so long. That will be the case for many footballers. I was just 29 years old when I quit the game and found it very difficult to know what to do next. I got a taste of what it would be like to drift through life without much purpose but then began to put together the pieces that became a new life. But some of these young people will not have the same financial motivation that drove me to find a new path. Some will come face to face with a very painful and lonely reality at what is still a relatively young age when they hang up their boots

Whereas we had the choice of mixing with ordinary people, they have become isolated as a result of their fame and wealth. You don't normally see celebrities and multi-millionaires socialising with everyday folk for very good reasons including their own personal security. Footballers are advised where they should or shouldn't go for their own good and it's causing them to live a life very remote from reality while still at a very young age.

This is also making it harder for them to form real, lasting relationships. To be honest, I don't know how they find proper girlfriends or wives. Ok, there have always been girls who go out and about looking for the company of footballers, but things have changed in very important ways. There were no camera phones in my day, or the thought that you could be going out with someone who could sell their story to the newspapers. So do I judge them when you read about footballers having a drink, getting involved in affairs or falling foul of the law? No, I don't. To do so would be very hypocritical because, whatever they do now, we did tenfold in my day.

Back then we got away with the vast majority of it and enjoyed almost every minute! Reports about footballers going out drinking, perhaps at a Christmas party, a pre-season break or other time in the season, annoy me. I know sports science paints a different picture on alcohol these days, but I still don't think there's anything wrong in going out for a pint with the lads. In fact I'd say it's a very good thing. Team spirit is very important. That doesn't just come from fighting for the same cause for 90 minutes on a Saturday but by spending time together socially as well. Going for a drink with team mates is a bonding exercise. As long as things don't get out of hand and players aren't going home drunk or out of control, I can't see the problem with it.

Having said all that, I don't think you'd find many of today's Premier League sides socialising together as we used to do. I'm not using this point as an excuse for slamming foreign players who have brought quality, variety and great entertainment to our domestic game, but modern dressing rooms are often full of cliques because you have players from different countries who naturally flock together rather than being part of a team.

I don't think you'd see today's multi-national, as well as multi-talented, Manchester City side socialising together except for a few formal club occasions. It's just another way, to be honest, in which today's game has changed but not necessarily for the better.

I'm not sure I'd have enjoyed myself quite as much as a hard-tackling defender in the modern climate. It's almost become a cliché that the art of tackling has gone out of the game, but that's because it is true. To me, there was no more exciting sight in football than true hard men such as Stuart Pearce and Pat Van Den Hauwe coming together full crunch in a bone jerking tackle. It was fantastic – an incident guaranteed to get fans up from their seats! You knew these guys were honest men going into battle. There was no quarter asked for or given and relatively few injuries when you consider they were playing a very physical game.

Could you ever imagine Psycho rolling around the pitch in agony? You'd have had to shoot him to see that. I know exactly how he was feeling because I was the same at heart, even if not quite as celebrated a player. Never in a million years would I want to let someone – my direct opponent being number one – see that I was hurt. Of course it would be agony, at times, when I emerged from a tackle but I didn't want to give away any feelings of weakness to my opponents or my team mates. If I'd gone down taking the mickey as players do nowadays, one of our lads would have hauled me back up and told me not to be such a wimp.

People go crazy these days about issues such as whether a tackle is slightly from behind, from the side or even with feet off the ground. What sort of game do they think we are supposed to be playing? Tackling, like everything else in football, is an art. I see tackles in most live games I cover that are actually great tackles which then result in either a yellow card and a strong lecture or even a straight red. But rarely do I see a player really getting injured by a good honest tackle. They may go down to draw the referee's attention to the incident but they're soon up on their feet and skipping away like a lamb when action has been taken in their favour.

Don't get me wrong, it wasn't a one-way street in my day with defenders kicking lumps out of innocent strikers. The treatment was more often 50-50. I came up against many forwards who could dish it out like the best of us. There was a mutual feeling of respect because such a physical challenge was expected. The forward I was marking knew I'd take advantage of my 'free one' and give him a reminder in the first few minutes that he was going to be in a game. Many strikers gave me one back as soon as possible to tell me I wasn't having it all my own way. Most of the time it was good, honest stuff.

Going into a tackle in a half-hearted fashion or just trying to nick the ball away from a striker is more likely to cause injury than a real red-blooded tackle. That's why friendlies can be a bit of a minefield. The best way has always been to commit yourself 100 per cent and be honest.

I'd like to see referees give defenders a break and allow them more freedom to tackle. Providing they are good at their job, they should be able to tell the difference between a player going all out for the ball and catching his man by mistake as opposed to deliberately injuring someone. In the same way, I'll always back myself to know when a player is really hurt. If a player stays still, you may have cause to worry. When they're rolling around, it's odds on they're just trying to get the referee's attention.

Such judgement comes from inside knowledge. If you've played the game to a reasonable level, you should be able to distinguish between what is real and what isn't. I'm not going to hold my breath though because today's game is going in a totally opposite direction and there's nothing any of us golden oldies can do about it!

The 'mateyness' between rival players today makes me cringe. From my view in the tunnel before the game I see players high-fiving each other and looking as if they are all best friends. Then they go through the on-pitch farce of shaking hands with opponents. Honestly, that's rubbish, in my opinion. I've even seen players from opposing sides swap shirts at half time. No wonder managers of lower sides sometimes worry that their players are too much in awe of the stars from the top clubs.

For my money, I'd recommend the semi-brawl between Roy Keane and Patrick Viera before a Manchester United versus Arsenal match as a better way of preparing for battle. I don't particularly want to see players fighting but they are going out there to take part in a proper contest, not to socialise. I was the first player to shake hands with an opponent after the final whistle once the match was done and dusted – and even go out for a drink with a lad who'd given me hell that afternoon. That's not a problem. But I honestly don't know why players are so friendly with each other before games. Perhaps it's because they are all in the same goldfish bowl away from the real world, and changing clubs so often that there's very little loyalty to their badge. But I don't like it.

I'm not keen either on the penalty area wrestling matches you see so often. I'm sure you know exactly what I mean. It's a free kick or a corner and you've got defenders with their arms around the waists of opposition players to ensure they don't get a run at the ball. Often officials view it as six-of-one and half-a-dozen of the other and almost impossible for them to make a decision. But they don't always have such an easy get-out clause. Like many millions, I looked forward to watching Scottish champions Celtic going head-to-head with Italian giants Juventus in the last 16 of the Champions League earlier this year. But I actually switched my TV off long before the final whistle. Like nearly everyone else, I'd seen Juve defenders manhandling Celtic's players in a ridiculous fashion. Neil Lennon's men couldn't get the ball in the back of the net that evening but I swear several of his players made it – after being pushed and almost wrestled into the goal.

The answer in such circumstances, is for the referee to issue a yellow card and a penalty. Even if he has to award two or three, it would still be the correct decision and would soon get the right message out to other clubs.

I don't always agree with everything the *Match of the Day* pundits say but I definitely give Liverpool stalwart Alan Hansen thumbs up for his comments about defending. To me, it looks as if the most important art of all in the game, preventing the opposition from scoring, seems to have been lost somewhere. Part of the problem seems to be the insistence of some coaches to use zonal marking. That's more like a suicide note than a defensive tactic. This is one reason why so many goals seem to be scored from corners in the modern game. I'm now seeing players turning their faces away from the ball, particularly when grappling with strikers in the way I've just described.

If I'd seen a Sheffield United player do that I'd have knocked his block off. The problem with zonal marking is that it gives forwards the chance to make a run and literally meet the ball head on. On many occasions, all a defender has to do is physically make a challenge to put the forward off. From a 50-50 jump, I'd expect to either get my head on the ball first or do enough to make life difficult for my opponent. But I wouldn't be nearly so confident trying to fend off a forward allowed to run unchecked a few yards and then jump. Imagine allowing the likes of big Andy Carroll to have that advantage? It's crazy.

Yes, there have been changes in the game but generally this remains a simple sport. It's eleven against eleven and either you have the ball or they have it. When you get the ball, move it around and keep it. When they have it, get it back as quickly as you can and try to win it. I know that sounds ridiculously easy, but that's how it is. The way I preferred to play and would still recommend to defenders today is to split the pitch down the middle as I did with John MacPhail. I was a left sided defender, so I would take that area and MacPhail would look after the other half.

This was better than simply choosing to mark the same player as it safeguarded us both from being dragged into areas of the pitch in which we weren't so comfortable. But when it came to defending set pieces and corners, we'd pick forwards up one-to-one and look after them. Then, if my forward scored, I was the one to blame, and if MacPhail's striker did the business, we knew to point the fingers at him. Everyone was accountable and knew exactly where they stood. Also, I see defenders in the modern game who just can't tackle. Appreciating the fact that defenders have to be even more careful about any contact in the penalty area, I see teams selecting what I would call 'athletes', particularly in the wide positions of either full back or wing back. But their lack of defensive appetite and ability is obvious to anyone with a trained eye.

When I hear a lot of talk about formations, some of which sound more like a mathematical puzzle compared to good old fashioned 4-4-2, it makes me laugh. I don't even agree with the idea of just playing one up front on his own with, sometimes, another forward just behind in the hole. In my day, strikers hunted in pairs – the top combinations I played against included Phil Boyer and Ted MacDougall, Trevor Francis and Kenny Burns, and Graeme Sharp and Adrian Heath.

In our Fourth Division title winning side, we had the partnership of Bob Hatton and Keith Edwards. My point is that, because they played together regularly and got to know each other's games, they became much more successful than they would if they'd played on their own. Where modern theorists are making a mistake, in my view, is by taking ideas employed by the very best sides at club and international level and trying to repeat that further down the pecking order. It's very tempting to say teams should all try to play like Barcelona and Spain, who at times during Euro 2012 didn't field a striker at all, but it just doesn't work like that. You have to be an exceptional player to play up front on your own or be part of a system that genuinely gets midfield or wide players up in support. Too often, I see teams going with just one striker and not looking like scoring if they played all week.

Without doubt, there have been welcome improvements in the modern game, with the way they now look after injuries being one of them. When a player is injured today, major clubs have access to medical expertise to diagnose quickly and accurately, offer the correct treatment, and then to organise a sensible recovery programme. Players soldiering on when they are suffering from real injuries are much rarer and we should all be grateful for that. Yet sports science has also brought a way of thinking that, for me, doesn't always make sense. When I hear managers complain their players are physically tired, I want to get up out of my chair, switch off the TV and shout 'bollocks' very loudly. Why can't more bosses just be honest and say they lost because of their own mistakes rather than make such ridiculous excuses?

Ok, I accept the pace of the game is much quicker, with the ball being in play longer and pitches generally being in far better condition. But they don't necessarily play more matches than we did and everything is laid on a plate. You'll often hear that one of the top sides had to travel to Europe in midweek and that supposedly causes problems when they play in the Premier League at the weekend. But these lads have been mollycoddled all the way along. They have jumped on a plane, enjoyed luxury travel in a coach and been put up in a top class hotel where they get the opportunity to rest before the match. What is so difficult or tiring about that?

I've got similar views on how sports science experts call the tune on recovery time. Teams are often rotating their players because of so-called fixture congestion, but aren't we overdoing it? Yes, it may well be that physically a player isn't 100 per cent recovered from going through a tough 90 minutes three or four days previously, but there's more to this game than that. It never went through my head when we had two matches on successive days against Southend and Sheffield Wednesday that I could only play in one of them. Adrenalin goes a long way to making up for any shortfalls in energy.

I lose count of the number of times I went into a match below full fitness but forgot about whatever was niggling me once I got immersed in the 90 minutes. It's all well and good for clubs such as Manchester United to rotate Wayne Rooney and Robin van Persie, you're talking about replacing one great player with another, and that isn't going to make too much difference to their goal potential. But when clubs further down the scale take the same ideas on board, such decisions become far more questionable.

Talking of tired old excuses, I hate the way the national side is treated these days. Being raised in the halcyon days of the 1960s when England won the World Cup, the contrast between the priority it was given then and now is stark. Much of this is down to Premier League clubs putting pressure on their stars to stay loyal to their main employers rather than turn out for their countries.

If I was manager of England, any club manager trying to tell me to rest one of his players or only play them for 45 minutes in a friendly would get a very short answer – the type that has only two words and ends in 'off'. Of course I realise that, in practice, it's very important for the England manager to be on good terms with club managers, but someone should lay down a marker that representing your country at the highest level of the game is the pinnacle of football. Or it should be.

I refer back to Jimmy Sirrel at Sheffield when I was a raw teenager seeking to make my way in the game. He could have put barriers in the way of Simon Stainrod and me when we were called up to play in a couple of international youth tournaments with England. But he didn't. Instead he told us it was an honour to play for your country – and how right he was. I may never have made it to the senior squad but putting on that England shirt was one of the proudest moments of my life. I'd have given anything to be named in any kind of England squad in the years that followed, let alone win myself another cap. So I find it very difficult when either young players turn down the opportunity to play in youth tournaments or senior lads pull out of full internationals.

Tell me, also, what is international retirement all about? How can a player decide he's had enough of representing his country even if it stretches him to his physical limits? It's totally beyond me, to be quite honest. That partly explains why the current England national side is not a patch on the 1966 squad. Winning that competition meant absolutely everything to those heroes who spent weeks in a team camp preparing for their dates with destiny.

Sadly, we're coming closer and closer to players not so much motivated by the glory of winning trophies and playing for their country but purely raking in more and more money. You can see this from the way the cup competitions are now being viewed by the clubs. Winning the FA Cup is regarded as cheap beer compared with finishing 17th in the Premier League and staying on the gravy trail. In the same way, players are often happy to see out contracts when they've got no chance of making the first team because they are being paid top dollar. That's the exact opposite to the way I felt and still feel about the game.

Part Two: Life

THERE have been two major influences in transforming the sometimes arrogant bachelor footballer into the proud family man I am today. First, although I would never have chosen it, was my time in prison. I was shaken completely out of my comfort zone, saw sights I never want to see again and discovered how desperate life can be inside. But in many ways it did me a hell of a lot of good.

Having started out as a down-to-earth lad from a council estate, almost starstruck when I first went into the professional football world at Sheffield United, I'd gone down the road of so many footballers by beginning to believe my own publicity. You get drawn into an unreal world as a footballer, a 'bubble', if you like. It comes from the money and the attention you get from the media and the fans. You tell yourself you are not going to let it get to you and you will remain the same person – but I'd defy almost anyone to do so.

Instead you do start to get arrogant, thinking you are someone special because of the way people treat you. With that mindset, it becomes easy to believe you can get away with almost anything because there's always someone else there to clear up the mess. I lived life to the full – and enjoyed a lot of it – but I probably needed bringing down a peg or two. I still think years on that I was the victim of a witch hunt, but I didn't help myself by not telling the truth. The police gave every impression that they'd livened up their Friday night by netting a well-known fish and all that time later the court also seemed as if it was making an example of me. In my defence, I'd say I was badly advised when it came to my plea and I'd handle it differently now. I'm a straight talking, honest guy by nature and I should have held my hand up and admitted I'd done wrong by not owning up to what was a fairly minor accident.

Yet going to prison and seeing how some other people lived, as far removed as you can imagine from the glamorous world of football, did me a favour in a way I could never have expected. It was my equivalent, if you like, of a few months in the army. In that hard world, I was no longer Tony Kenworthy, the footballer, but Tony Kenworthy, the human being. I was treated just like everyone else.

In prison, the baseline is that they regard you as scum and respect has to be earned, not given. I drew deep on my basic principles of working hard, the beliefs my parents had instilled in me all those years previously. I honestly think I left those two prisons a better and wiser person. I became less judgemental and started to treat people better, because I'd learnt how easy it is for someone to hit rock bottom. Realising how quickly everything can be taken away, I became far more grateful for having a life I'd begun to take for granted.

The other change came about from meeting Jacqueline. Having lived a far different life in Sheffield, I met her at an absolutely crucial time in my life when I could so easily have gone downhill very quickly. The reality of ceasing to be a footballer was beginning to hit me. I'd split up with my girlfriend Michelle and faced a number of situations that led me to seriously wonder where my life was heading.

Being shown the door at Bramall Lane and Mansfield Town, going to prison, then the mixed experiences with Reg that eventually led me into a working cul-de-sac, meant I was extremely vulnerable to dark days ahead. Physically I knew I was going to have to live with the consequences of constantly putting my body on the line on the football field and mentally I faced a real battle to see how I could ever live without the highs of playing for 90 minutes in front of thousands of people every week. It was so tempting to hit the bottle but that just makes things worse – you wake up feeling rough with the problems you're trying to avoid still there. But just when I could make a case for feeling sorry for myself, a woman came into my life who had a very different perspective. Not having any experience of football meant she could tell me to man up, get a grip and open my eyes to the fact I was a young man in my 30s with a hell of a lot of life ahead of me. It might seem a strange thing to say from a man who unashamedly fell in love with Sheffield as a city, but permanently basing myself in the North East has also been very good for me as it helped me to make a brand new start.

Everything about Jacqueline as a person is good for me. She is a much calmer person than I am, not letting anything upset her too much and not taking things too seriously. She is also very funny, another reason I was instantly attracted to her. Jacqueline, who has worked for the probation service for about 25 years, has a very caring personality. It's good for me that she isn't a football fan and had no idea who I was when we first got to know each other before things blossomed into a close relationship.

I was working in football with Darlington and because of the way people spoke to me when we were out, she soon enough got an idea I may be known for my sport. She left it to me to tell her about my career as a footballer and she responded mostly with a shrug of the shoulders. I could have been upset about that but it was quite nice that she didn't think it was a big deal. She did have some idea of a sportsman's lifestyle as her brother-in-law is Steve Hackney, the former Leicester Tigers rugby player and she has become proud of what I achieved on the football field before we met. She also thoroughly enjoys our trips, two or three times a year, to Bramall Lane and the way the club treats the whole family.

My point is that Jacqueline's personality and way of looking at life has rubbed off on me. My nature is to be more pushy and up front. My father told me from an early age that because of my tendency to call a spade a spade and tell people exactly what I thought, I'd not make many friends – and he wasn't far off the truth. But I'd rather be that way than talk behind someone's back. In fact, I often tell people to act in the same way and that if they are going to tell me something, they better say the same to the person they are talking about. I can't stand people who do the opposite. They include folk who are more than happy to load the gun, then leave you in the lurch by backing off or keeping quiet when the argument they have provoked takes place.

I thought I was better than some other people when I was a professional footballer when I was really just a lad off a Leeds council estate who could play the game better than most of his peers. But, firstly through my months in prison and then again through meeting Jacqueline, I have changed for the better. In particular, I've become more patient with people and they are what really matter in this world. I will stop and chat and treat others with more understanding and respect.

When I think back, I can see times when I was a complete arse for not giving fans the time of day when I wasn't in the mood. I failed to take on board during my playing days how quickly my football career would pass, and that afterwards I'd find people not so likely to recognise me or want to talk with me. Particularly because I live a fair trek from Sheffield and years have now passed, I'm not so instantly recognisable anymore. Some folk recall me from my Blades days and talk, but plenty just know me from the guy I've become since.

My children, Sophie and Wil, also know me as a father rather than a footballer, which again I think is a good thing. There's more evidence of Wayne Rooney and Steven Gerrard and co in my son's bedroom than of Tony Kenworthy, Yet he too enjoys the odd moments when he finds out about my career. Quite recently he was really excited when I got a mention on a TV show for being picked in someone's all-time Blades XI. That gave him a thrill but he doesn't go around telling others that his father was a professional. He just gets on with things quietly without any fuss. Wil has more of his mother's personality than mine. He'll shrug things off rather than get involved in a confrontation and concentrate on what he is doing.

I'm very, very proud of both my children. Sofie is a natural athlete who runs for her school. Personality-wise, she is much more like me. She doesn't suffer fools gladly and sums people up very quickly, usually getting them just right. She'll probably face the same challenges as I did socially but will be able to sleep soundly at night knowing she has been true to herself. Both children are very intelligent and we don't have to push them to get on with their homework when they come home. They are young people with good heads on their shoulders and good futures. They contribute a lot to a house that is hardly ever quiet. There's always something happening in one of the rooms – it's a home rather than a house, I'm glad to say, with a lot for me as a father to get involved with. It's all hustle and bustle and helps keep me young.

There could even be another Kenworthy on a prominent football shirt before too long in Wil. Like his Dad, he's a forward at this age and banging in more than his fair share of goals in the TJFA Premier Division, which is a very reasonable standard. The last thing I'd ever do would be to put pressure on him because anything can happen in a young person's footballing development, but he has more natural ability than I had at the same age. Already scouts are sniffing around him so we will just have to wait and see.

What I don't want to see is Wil ending up in one of the club academies because I don't believe in them at all. To me, they're taking lads at too young an age and writing many of them off. It is even harder to make it to the top level now than it was in my day, so it is great that Wil is also a very clever lad who is doing well with his studies. But, yes, I would recommend the life of a pro to him, as I would to any similarly talented young man with football in his blood. Never mind the financial rewards, it's a great sport for building up life skills and will leave you with a mountain of memories. He's a Manchester United and Boro fan by nature, although Dad is always nudging him towards the Blades. He thoroughly enjoys our visits to Bramall Lane and will always support the red and white wizards when he sees them. In fact, he has worn a Blades shirt, although not necessarily by choice. Every now and again I go into his bedroom in the night and dress him in a Sheffield United top. He'll then wake up in the morning and know Dad has been up to his tricks again.

I certainly wouldn't mind swapping this older injury-hit body for a younger, fitter one. Like many players from my generation, I will carry battle scars from my football career to the grave. It's a good job only my wife Jacqueline gets to witness my early morning routine. Just getting out of bed is horrendous. It's a major, lengthy and very painful operation most folk of my age – I celebrate my 55th birthday on 30 October, 2013 – take for granted. I'm not writing this to make you feel sorry for me or because I want a medal. Nor am I in the business of regrets or trying to point a finger of blame at anyone. I just want you to know the whole truth about how football has affected my life for better and, in this case, for worse.

Biggest problem first thing is my left ankle which has been operated on three times and is basically shot to pieces. Getting that moving again each morning is very, very difficult. It takes a big, big effort just to get out of bed without being doubled up in agony and up to an hour before the ankle's warmed up enough for me to walk properly. That's not to mention my broken back, clicking knee and a face partly numb on my right hand side. I live with daily medication and painkillers, knowing something as innocuous and routine as a sneeze can jolt my back so badly I have no choice but to go to bed for a couple of days.

All in all, I'm a near physical wreck at an age when most folk have a fair few miles left on the clock. Boy, my wife must love me to put up with all that!

All those problems are a direct result of playing football. Commentators trot out phrases like 'putting his body on the line' or 'breaking his neck for the team', but I get the impression neither they nor the fans think about what really goes on. Such talk is fairly meaningless when applied to getting yourself in the way of a shot or going on a long run up the field. I'm talking about the times when my body was in such a painful and frightening mess, I had to ask myself very honestly whether it could possibly be worth months of lonely hard work to get back onto the football field again – but, yes, I'd do it even now, if I could.

If I have one regret – my failure to read Howard's letter apart – it's that I wish I'd taken time to draw breath and enjoy my playing career even more than I did. When you're at a football club there's a danger you'll start to regard it like doing a job. That's a mistake in my book. There's nothing normal or run-of-the-mill about being well paid to play the sport you love. There are thousands of good folk in the stands every Saturday afternoon who'd give their right arm to swap places with you, even just for a single 90 minutes. If you are playing football now, do yourself a favour and just take it all in whilst you can because, like my career, it really will be gone in a flash.

I'd like to close, however, with something even more important. For all my love of the Blades and football, life has taught me one invaluable lesson – family and friends are far more important. I have been so fortunate in recent years to discover that truth all over again. Kicking a football around a pitch is great but being around people you love is really what this strange life is all about.

I had the great benefit of being brought up by two fantastic people who gave me every encouragement to make the most of my talents and even more vitally, didn't judge me when I was at my lowest ebb and backed me purely because I was their son. Friends, and I'm talking about true friends, have also been there for me in the bad days as well as the good. They've helped to teach me many lessons. Now, in the the second half of my life, I've found a new family – the lasting joy of being with the woman I love and a father figure to two very special young people. My future is based on something more secure than the bounce of a football.

Thank you for reading my story and best wishes.

About the Authors

EVERY FAN looks for a footballer who truly shares their exclusive passion – Sheffield United's TONY KENWORTHY was that man in the golden era of the 1970s and 80s.

Brought up on a council estate in Leeds, TK joined the Blades as a schoolboy and kissed the badge for more than a decade before a succession of stomach-churning injuries forced him dragging and screaming out of Bramall Lane after his testimonial. Unexpected but glorious Wembley success followed at Ian Greaves' homely Mansfield Town before Tony was sent to prison after a minor road accident and experienced people and sights that reshaped the second half of his life.

Tony's story: *Blade Heart* reflects his down-to-earth character as he bares his soul relating the good times and bad in his emotive, rollercoaster life, on and off the football pitch.

AFTER working with Owls cult hero Terry Curran in *Regrets of a Football Maverick*, Sheffield-based writer JOHN BRINDLEY crosses the Steel City divide to bring you the story of Tony Kenworthy, the Blade Heart who fought Curran tooth-and-nail on the pitch during the epic derbies of 1979-80.

John is a football supporter and newspaper reporter who shares his love of the game through writing the life stories of South Yorkshire's iconic characters, beginning with Donny Rovers chairman John Ryan in 2010.

He says: 'Tony was a complete delight to work with. He speaks and lives with the same uncompromising honesty with which he played. He could have been a First Division player with any number of clubs but he was fiercely loyal to Sheffield United. Every club should have a TK at its core.'